The plight of Rwandese refugees after the genocide

The story of a survivor

From the middle of the Rwandese genocide to the heart of the United States

Ange Rukundo

<u>Dedications</u>

I dedicate this memoir to:

My dear mother who has been by my side throughout this hard journey,

My sister with whom we shared the same pains and joys,

My dear wife who lived a similar story,

My father,

My brother,

My twin sister of whom I, unfortunately, do not know the fate,

My little brother who did not survive the hard experience,

Jean-Claude Padot whose support helped me to write the first pages of this story,

Jacqueline Picoche whose help is the cornerstone of this work,

All refugees and especially Rwandan refugees scattered around the world,

And to all those who are fighting for a peaceful world and for the well-being of refugees who are far away from their homes.

PREFACE

By Jacqueline Picoche,

Linguist and Honorary Lecturer at University of Picardie, France

It is the internet that brought us together Ange and me, years ago. I was in my apartment in Paris and him in a small studio in the suburb of Bangui. We only met once, whereas, with a US passport, he stopped in Paris returning from Rwanda, his homeland. He was about 8 years old in 1994, the year of the Rwandan genocide and the beginning of his exodus; he was about 13 in 1999, when he arrived in Central African Republic and 21 in 2007, when he left for the United States. So it is between 1999 and 2007 that we corresponded assiduously. On arrival in Bangui he meets a "European Catholic priest" who "presents Mass for those who still believe" and survive untold dramas, and strives to "bring hope to their lives." Hope is reborn in fact: the work that his mother found in a French medical facility and scholarships of the High Commissioner for Refugees provide sustenance to three members of the survivors and united family, himself, his mother and younger sister. They are finally safe! Relative safety, because they had to take refuge at the Institut Pasteur in a French family, during the riots that accompanied, in 2001, a failed coup against President Patassé. Ange Rukundo during this period, he was asking me for advice and corrections for a variety of texts: this story, and several novels whose very current subjects, had much interest. Those novels, Mr. Rukundo, if you ever want to publish them, and God willing, I can give them a more academic figure, but it is not our problem today.

So I learned that Ange Rukundo's schooling was suspended for few years when fleeing through the particularly traumatic Africa, and that as soon as it was possible, he resumed his studies and put double efforts to cover the holes and catch up the delay. He got caught up at the point that he obtained in 2005 a math-physics high school diploma. And then, in the margins of all he has to learn (including Sango, the local African language), outside the small jobs that allow him to earn some money, he becomes a writer! And a writer in French! I was struck by the energy, intelligence, love of study, storytelling talent of this young man. I encouraged and advised him, and I certainly am touched by his acknowledgments. But finally this story clearly bears the mark of his sensitivity, his ability to tell the most dramatic episodes. It is his work. And now he asks me to fix it again, assuring me that he is free to change what he wants to his text, the book is printed on demand.

Hey! Well, I say no!

And I am sure that a famous contemporary novelist would agree with me. Michel Houellebecq, doesn't he write in the first pages of Submission, "a writer, is first of all a human being, present in his books. He writes very well or very poorly, ultimately, does not matter, the key is that he writes, and is actually present in his books. "

I affirm that Ange Rukundo is "present in his book."

Certainly, from his early childhood, he lives in a more or less bilingual society, and French, the official language, vehicular language with people of other ethnic groups, is taught in school. But, his mother tongue is Kinyarwanda, not French. French mixed with Sango that he learns end practices at school in Bangui is not exactly that of Louis Le Grandt or Janson de Sailly. Therefore, the result is a perfectly clear narrative, alive, exciting, without any annoying darkness. He bears the mark of a life shattered by the tragic events, his own life and that of the entire African continent. Leave the "rough around the edges," as they say in a concrete architecture, do not sand, and do not coat it. Do not forget that since 2007, the author lives in Denver (Colorado). French is not the official or commonly used language, but English, a language syntactically and phonetically so different! Learning English, mastering English, without losing his French is what he managed to do.

Fixing everything that would be marked "incorrect" copying a French person from France, born on educated French-speaking parents, would be a painstaking job that would lead to the impression that the text was written by a Parisian. You are not a Parisian, Ange Rukundo! You are a Rwandese francophone who became a citizen of the United States. This is your identity. It should be retained and you can be proud of. Besides being an Anglo-French-Sango-Kinyarwanda multilingual in this country, you have an asset that you may be able to use on occasions. That is what I wish for you and I see a bright future for you if you know how to seize your chances.

January 2015

Table of Contents

Chapter 1

Word on Rwanda and the author

Hills in Rwanda

It is in East Africa that we find this "country of a thousand hills," one of the countries that depicts the charm of Africa with its rivers, valleys, plains and numerous heavenly hills. Rwanda has an area of about 26,338 square kilometers (about 10,170 square miles) almost the size of Haiti. Rwanda enjoys almost a tropical climate due to its geographical location. The country is barely visible on the map because of its location right next to the giant ex-Zaire (Democratic Republic of Congo) in the West. Rwanda also shares a border with Uganda to the north, Burundi to the south and Tanzania to the south-east. The country attracts many tourists due to its hills that many Europeans compare to the Swiss hills; to tall volcanoes including the tallest, *Karisimbi*, which rises up to 4,500 meters (about 14,760 feet); to the mountain gorillas who are becoming rare in other parts of the world. Rwanda has many more beauties of nature that make the country attractive. Rwanda has often been cited among the countries of high population density. Despite its small size, Rwanda had a population of about eight million people in 1994.

Volcanoes in Rwanda

I am from an average African family of five children. In the years that preceded the events of 1994, we live a modest life. We eat and drink when we want to. We have a beautiful house that my father built during his youth. My mother has a good job in a tire store well known in the town of Kigali. My father has a good job as a technician-mechanic in a private company. My older brother, twin sister, little sister and I attend school daily. We attend the school called "Sainte Famille" which is located about ten miles from home, almost in the center of the city of Kigali. We get up every day early to go to school; we eat a delicious breakfast prepared by the lovely housekeeper. Then, we jump in my father's car which drops us at the bus stop where we wait impatiently with other students for the long green bus of the local transportation company *ONATRACOM*. In short, everything is well in my family and in most Rwandese families until 1994.

In the next chapter I will briefly talk about the history of Rwanda and about some precursors and the origin of the genocide as histrory tells us. I will not get into the historical details. Readers who are more interested in the history of Rwanda may consult books or works produced by experts and researchers.

In this book, I will focus on the events that I and many Rwandese refugees personally experienced after the Rwandese genocide of 1994.

Chapter 2

Events at the origine and Precursors of the genocide

History tells us that during the colonial era and before, the minority ethnic group Tutsi rules almost continuously over most of the territory. Kings, masters, officers and riches are mostly Tutsi, while most of the majority Hutu ethnic group people are farmers and servants. This disparity has benn worsened over the years by colonizers of Rwanda: Germany and Belgium. They promote the development of ideologies and practices leading to divisions and separations between those two main ethnic groups o Rwanda. Some examples of ideologies consist of spreading the idea that Tutsis are superior to Hutu in different ways. Some practices have consisted of strengthening and/or promoting the power or domination of the Tutsi ethnic group over the Hutu ethnic group. Therefore, in this colonial period, more Tutsi (the minority group) and less Hutus (the majority group) have access to education. This situation may have been the cause, or one of the causes, of rising tensions between the two ethnic groups, leading to the Rwandan Revolution of 1959.

That year marked a turning point in the unfolding of the history of

Rwanda in the 19th and 20th centuries. That year is the tipping point between the pre- and post-colonial era. In 1959, Rwanda is still under Belgian rule. The revolution begins with the attack by a group of Tutsi in 1959 on a Hutu politician Dominique Mbonyumutwa, who was the first President of Rwanda after the abolition of the Tutsi monarchy and the access of the country to independence. This incident sets fire to the powder and triggers an angry Hutu emancipation movement against the Tutsi population. This may have been the first violent conflict between the two ethnic groups. Many Tutsis were killed and thousands more fled to neighboring countries: Congo, Burundi, Tanzania and Uganda. A similar scenario is repeated three decades later in 1994, but this time, it is the Hutus people who will flee to the same neighboring countries.

Rwanda eventually gains its independence in 1962. The first government of the independent Rwanda, led by a Hutu President, is almost exclusively composed by Hutus. In the following years, the exiled Tutsi refugees in neighboring countries begin to carry out attacks in regions at the norther border, which results in repression against the Tutsi survivors who remained in Rwanda. In 1973, the Hutu President Juvenal Habyarimana seizes power by a military coup.

Around 1987, some members of the elite Tutsi refugees in neighboring countries create, in Uganda, the RPF movement (Rwandese Patriotic Front) which seeks the return of Tutsi refugees in Rwanda. This movement later gives birth to the Rwandan Patriotic Army (RPA), which is officially responsible for many of the attacks in Rwanda from 1990 to the 1994 genocide. In October 1990, the northern region of the country that became a regular target of the APR plunges into a war that gradually infects other areas. In July 1992, in the northeast of the country, fights between RPA rebels and government forces cause the displacement of about 300,000 people of both ethnic groups to other regions of the country. Among the displaced are thousands of Burundese refugees who were settled in Rwanda after the 1972 events in their country of Burundi.

Insecurity begins to reign almost everywhere in the country. Unidentified people place explosives in bus stations, schools, taxis and markets. Isolated incidents begin to be part of the daily lives of Rwandese people. Hidden weapons are discovered here and there.

I remember a night that we spend in panic when gunfire exchanges are heard in our district for a long hour. It is around nine in the evening when we are getting ready to sleep. During these gunfire exchanges, heavy weapons are heard and many people think that Kigali, the capital, is under attack because other northern regions are already regular targets since 1990. It was only the next morning that we learn what happened. There were few people dead. We are informed that it was a group of rebels secretly carrying weapons from the neighboring country Uganda towards the center of Kigali. They were surprised by a patrol on a routine check, and the rebels opened fire. This event causes fear among Kigali residents who are warned from that time on.

All this shows how the country is sinking deeper into the chaos that will lead it to disaster. During the following four years that the country experiences numerous attacks, isolated incidents, suspicions, fears and uncertainties about tomorrow; hatred between the two major groups that inhabit Rwanda increases on all levels. This hatred is already affecting the cultural, social and political domains despite countless negotiations and interventions of local, regional and foreign pacifists. New political parties are born and are trying to solve the political and security problems the country faces. While on one side there are organized meetings, negotiations and agreements to save the peace (Arusha Accords in Tanzania, 1993 for example); on the other side, weapons are brandished and hatred among people swells. Finally in 1994, furor overflows and the country sinks into all-out violence. This period's events are similar to 1959 events when the death of many Tutsi was preceded by an incident against an important Hutu politician. This time the coup against the Hutu President Juvenal Habyarimana is the cause.

Chapter 3

Assassination of the President

Beginning of the genocide

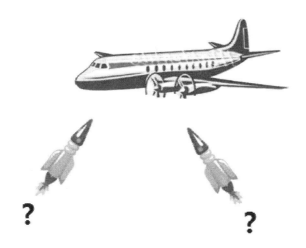

The presidential airplane is shot

     We are on Tuesday, April 6, 1994. The sun has set three hours ago after a long sunny day of scorching heat. It is about half past eight in the evening. The capital of Rwanda smells horror. A stunning and mesmerizing lull covers the city of Kigali despite the low hum of a few cars that still circulate in the deserted streets. Suddenly, the silence is broken by a little noise that rises from far away and begins to grow. It is the sound of a heavy engine of a plane flying over the city at a low altitude toward the airport Kayibanda, named in memory of the second president who led Rwanda after independence. Two minutes have not yet elapsed when three distant and spaced explosions are heard.

     We are not surprised at all because hearing those kinds of gunshots and isolated explosions has become part of our everyday life. We are already used to it. Certainly tomorrow morning we will learn in newspapers, as usual, that the gunshots of last night killed many innocent people and wounded many others. Plunged back into our endless thoughts and fears for tomorrow, we are listening to the local traditional music broadcasted almost every night on national radio. This music helps people forget the horrors of the day and get to sleep. Suddenly an unusual, hoarse and monotonous male voice interrupts the relaxing music that is already making us sleepy. Without even apologizing for the interruption, the voice whispers something we at first do not believe: the airplane that was bringing the President back home from a peace talk meeting in Tanzania has been shot in the quiet and dark sky of Kigali! The same voice continues the transmission of the bad news.

Doubts, misunderstanding and fear spread to those who just heard this news. Worried comments begin to circulate by word of mouth. People increase the volume of their radios to better hear what is being said. Some try to get foreign radio channels such as the French radio RFI or the London BBC in order to be better informed about the events, but it seems like the news has not yet spread abroad. We want to phone friends and colleagues to ask them if they heard the same news, but our hands are shaking and our heart are throbbing.

Half an hour later, many people still do not believe what has just been announced on the Rwandese national radio while others already understand the event and have began to predict what horror is to come. Some of those who closely followed the evolution of political events in Rwanda in recent months are not surprised because they knew that something dramatic was inevitable. "We do not even have extra food set aside in the house!" some moms whisper to their husbands while dads have their ears glued to radios. Most children are already sleeping and those who are still awake do not understand what is happening.

That night marks the beginning of the darkest period in the history of this small country. The events that will sadly make Rwanda known to the world and whose consequences will heavily weight on the future of this country and its people. A dark spot that will always be on a page of this country's history.

Even now, 20 years later, historical versions still contradict each other about what really happened that night of April 6, 1994. Two parties blame each other for the assassination of President Juvenal Habyarimana. Investigations to uncover the truth never succeeded or never made the results public.

On one side was the Tutsi Rwandese Patriotic Army in exile that had led several attacks against Rwanda, that had vigorously imposed itself on the political scene in previous years, and which would probably benefit the most from the death of the President. This movement denies responsibility for the fatal shot fired on the presidential airplane. This RPF blames Hutu extremists and some members of the Hutu government whom it believes would have preferred to kill the President rather than see him favorable to negotiations with rebels. A small detail to add is that there was little likelihood for the Tutsi minority, less than 30% of the population in those days, to come to power by means of democratic elections. And a large part of that minority was exiled outside of the country. Therefore, for a Tutsi regime to come to power, it would have to go against the rules of democracy!

On the other side, the Hutu government in mourning accuses the rebels of killing the President, the supreme commander of the army, in their attempt to weaken the legitimate army in order to seize power. The RPF rebels could not obtain everything they want or require, as long as the highest function of the country is not carried on by one of their own.

President Habyarimana before his death may have desperately dedicated himself to the task of establishing peace between rebel leaders and some members of his own government. He had responded to several calls from many peacemakers and presidents in the region. Some of them pressured him while others were advising him to negotiate or share the power with the rebels. This is a complex political subject that I do not wish to discuss here.

However, what many Rwandese people know is that the worst of the Rwandese story begins just after the assassination of the President. The Hutu militia which according to some sources, is organized and supported by some influential members of the government in mourning, engages in targeted killings against the Tutsi population and moderate Hutus. Most people who are killed in the first few weeks are the Tutsi; they are either killed only because they are Tutsi or because they are spies or because they are part of the rebellion. Moderate Hutus are also killed either because they are spies for the rebels or because they are opposed to the government. Once again, I do not wish to comment more about what really happened since I do not have reliable information about the facts, but books have been written and will be written about this humanitarian tragedy that regional and international media will talk about for many years to come.

A cemetery of victims in 1994

While people cry, moan and die, the Rwandese Patriotic Army composed exclusively of Tutsi, motivated by rage and seeking revenge, takes advantage of the weakening of the Hutu government, the beheading of the government army, the disorder and fear that exist to conduct monstrous attacks that leave death on their way. At this time while some Hutu are killing Tutsi inside Rwanda, the Tutsi rebel army advances to conquer the country, killing Hutus either because they are Hutu or because they are accused of killing the Tutsi rebels' brothers.

Rebels

Chapter 4

The beginning of the exodus

A long and hard week for the country just ended. It is desolation; the blood flows! People are stuck in their homes. A few starving and brave civilians leave their homes to look for food despite the danger. Food supplies are running out, gunshots are increasing and it is not clear who is shooting who and why.

The neighborhood in which we lived

It is April 12 around seven in the morning. Our house is located in a suburb of Kigali, about ten kilometers from the center of the city. Because there has been no school for a week, I wake up every morning to take care of the chickens, ducks and rabbits we raise at home and which we have been eating in the last seven days because we cannot go to the market. Immersed in my work, I hear from our neighbors some confused conversations in which I am able to pick up the last words: "Get out quickly and flee because they are already there." Despite my young age, those do not sound right in my head. The context of war in which we live in causes me to take these words seriously. After thinking about them for a few seconds, I decide to go back inside the house and tell them to my father. I knock on my parents' bedroom door. They were still sleeping. When my father, half asleep, opens the door, I repeat to him the words I just heard. After hearing them, he looks straight into my eyes for few seconds to detect if I am lying or joking. Then he tells me, "Go back to sleep!" I did not know that I said these words so loudly that my mother heard them. While my father tries to sink back into sleep, my mother is thinking about the words she just heard from me. Frightened by her thoughts, she urges my father to go out and learn what is happening. Unwillingly, my father rises heavily and heads toward the gate in our yard. He opens it and slips outside. He begins to walk along the small deserted street towards the main road. The gunshots have stopped; even the swallows that wake us up every morning with their beautiful songs are not singing. Such calm in times of war in the suburbs of the capital certainly conceals surprises we would soon learn about!

My father has not even gone twenty yards when he is nearly struck by a man who arises from nowhere. He is running and out of breath. My father immediately recognizes him as our neighbor who lives about a hundred meters from us. Upon seeing my father, he shouts "What are you still doing here? The rebels are already here!" Before this man finishes his sentence, my father already understands. He returns home in haste, opens the gate and without even entering, he shouts. "Get out of the house and flee toward the West" He adds nothing then disappears.

The alert is given and it is up to us to save ourselves. My mother, who is still lightly sleeping and immersed in her deep thoughts, hears these distant words of my father. Still in her night gown, she jumps and runs towards the baby who is peacefully asleep in his cradle like a little angel. At the same time, I run through all the rooms waking up my siblings.

"What's the matter with you? Are you crazy!" they scream at me. I only take five seconds to explain to them the situation. This is the first time such a thing has happens to us. We do not know what to do! Everyone grabs a small backpack and puts whatever they can reach. We are running all over the house shouting and seeking what can be most useful. Unfortunately, everything seems useful and we don't know what to take or what to leave behind! Three minutes later, we are locking the doors of the house and leaving through the small gate in the backyard.

The neighborhood is so empty and quiet that you'd think it is a cemetery. I think we are the last people to leave the neighborhood. We are leaving our home thinking that we will be back in a few hours or days without knowing we are leaving for good. We are lucky we ran away early before it was too late. Not far from our house, about a kilometer away, was a family who was unaware of the rebels' arrival. According to later testimonies, that family was surprised by the rebels who entered the house and killed the entire family who were still sleeping. If I did not wake up early that morning, if I had not heard those words from neighbors, if I had ignored them or if my mother had not heard them or urged my father to stand up, maybe we would not have made it out alive. My family and I would certainly have had the same fate that many families have known when they were surprised by rebels whose strategy was to surprise their victims.

After walking—almost running—a few meters, we come to the main road that is full of a crowd of refugees in disarray. Some of them have empty hands and others have had time to collect a few belongings that they carry on their heads. Women are dragging their crying children behind them; the children cry for their mothers to abandon the baggage in order to carry them on their backs. There is no talk among the adults; we can only hear the screaming, the crying of children and the sounds of hurried footsteps that devour the road. We have just started the first day of long years of our flight and exile in search of a peaceful retreat.

My father is already gone and we don't know where. But as he told us to flee westward, surely he knows what road we are taking because there is only one main road and hopefully he is waiting for us ahead. A few kilometers from our home is a vehicle repair shop in which my father had once worked (he was a mechanic for years). This shop has been abandoned by its owners and is empty except for few vehicles that have mechanical problems. Passing by the shop, my father tells himself that if he enters, he may find a vehicle that can possibly be quickly repaired and that might help us move quicker and further. He enters through the shop gates, walks in and looks around. He notices with disappointment a few vehicles in deplorable conditions.

Disappointed, he is getting ready to leave the shop when he sees a yellow minibus in the far corner of the shop. After a quick inspection, he realizes that the vehicle has three wheels and a rim. Of course the vehicle's key is not there. The vehicle did not even have a spare tire and my father did not have time to look for one to replace it. After few maneuverings, he manages to start the car engine. With its three wheels and the rim, the minibus starts moving forward!

The minibus like the one my father found

Once on the road, my father starts looking for us among a crowd of refugees in a hurry on the road. When he sees people that he knows among the refugees, he asks them if they saw us. He learns that we have advanced a little further, so he continues looking for us ahead. A moment later, he finds us walking among other refugees. We have just gone about five kilometers since we left home but we feel like we have just traveled the whole world on foot, and yet this is only the beginning!

The inibus making its way among refugees

My mother, sisters, brothers and I jump in the small bus and since it is not full yet, my father invites other refugees to join us and occupy all the empty seats or spaces that remained. Refugees hurry and scramble to climb into the bus that fills up immediately. The van starts to move slowly, honking to clear a way through this crowd of men, women and children frightened and moving. Some of them desperately try to hold on to the minibus which unfortunately is already full to bursting while others are begging us not to abandon them. I am terrified by the sight of such a large crowd of people fleeing in a stampede. I want to help but I am not able to. I feel pity for them; but also for us because I fear for what will happen to us. At this moment, I barely understand why we all are running away and from what.

When we arrive at a checkpoint erected by government forces on the deck of the Nyabarongo River, we are stopped by the military that still patrol some parts of the country not yet conquered by the rebels. We learn that this checkpoint aims to control people who are fleeing to prevent the rebels' mingling with refugees and quickly infiltrating other parts of the country. This will happen eventually but at least the course of events will be slowed, allowing a large number of refugees to save their lives.

We all are invited to get out of the vehicle and allow the soldiers to conduct a search. Noting the state of the vehicle in which we were riding, they order us to repair the vehicle before we can get back on the road. They give my father a used tire to place on the minibus. Fifteen minutes later, my father finally replaces the tire that was missing and now the vehicle is in good condition to hit the road! We jump in the bus again and without wasting time, we immediately get on the road for a long journey towards the south-west of the country, to the town of Gitarama. Since the north part of the country borders with Uganda where the rebels came from, is already under rebels' control, most people are fleeing towards the East, South or West of the country.

Our first destination

Chapter 5

Refugees at my grandfather's

After driving several tens of kilometers towards the south-west, in this small bus where it is boiling hot despite the gusts of wind that enter the bus, we arrive in the town of Gitarama located about 45 kilometers from the capital of Kigali. It is about noon. The city is sunny. The other refugees, who were on the bus, get off, thank my father and take different directions. Crowds of refugees in cars, on motorcycles, bicycles and foot enter the city every hour from Kigali. The rebels are not yet officially here in Gitarama. It is time for us to rest, look for something to eat and review the events that have just happened!

What a coincidence! We haven't even been here an hour when my father runs into the owner of the minibus that brought us here. He is also a refugee in this little town where he arrived this morning. My father happens to have met him a couple of months earlier. They then spend the following hour talking about the course of events that are taking place in the country. Finally the man takes his minibus and thanks my father for bringing it. Now, we do not have a car to move us and we have not yet reached our destination for the day. We need to travel about two dozen kilometers in order to get to my grandfather's house in one of the surrounding provinces.

The evening is falling in a couple of hours and the sun is starting to go down. We cannot return to Kigali yet as fights still rage between the rebel army that wants to take over the power and the government army that resists. We decide to take a taxi and go to my grandfather's.

At our arrival, we are greeted at the same time as refugees and family members. It is here at my grandfather's home that we will spend the following days. Every day we try to learn about the course of events in order to prepare ourselves to return home once peace returns.

A couple of months pass. In July, after several days of intense fighting between government forces and rebels, we learn that Kigali, the capital, fell into the hands of the rebels. The Hutu government that had already taken refuge in the north-west of the country crosses the border towards Goma in Congo. After the capital, the Tutsi rebellion begins to conquer the rest of the country. For us this means that we must prepare for a new flight.

We start noticing that the neighboring provinces are decreasing in population every day. People leave their homes and run away as the army of the new regime in Kigali progresses toward other parts of the country. The frightening news reaches us about the massacres that this army is conducting.

Chapter 6

Fleeing toward Congo

[Note: From now on I will use "we" to mean me, my family and other refugees. In instances where "we" refers to me and my family only, I will clarify.]

One morning we learn that the district where we are located is an imminent rebel attack target. We tell ourselves that this is just one of those damn rumors that we are used to hearing every day. But it does not take long before we find out that we are wrong.

We are in the afternoon. Suddenly, we hear gunshots and explosives in the far distance. This is the first time we hear gunshots since leaving Kigali, a little over two months earlier. This is an alarm sound for us. It is time to pack and leave!

An hour later, our district is beset. Bullets fly everywhere. We feel like our home is the main target because we hear bullets striking the roof and explosives blowing up around the house. We must get out of the house as soon as possible. But we do not know what direction to take once outside because we do not know where the bullets are coming from or where they are going. Moments later, we are crawling through bushes. I don't even remember how we got out of the house! We are trying to move as far away as we can from this battlefield and as quickly as we can. We learn later on that a resistance cell that had settled on a small hill right behind our house was fighting against the army in conquest of the country that was positioned on the other hill. And we were caught in the middle.

By the grace of God, my family and I are able to escape. With a few pieces of luggage that we are able to carry, we are walking in a hurry, crossing valleys, savannahs and plains with other displaced people. We are able to flee with our grandfather who is more than seventy-five years old. Tired from walking and under the weight of age, my grandfather decides to turn around and go back, saying, "If it is time to die, I am already old anyway and prefer to die in my own house, on the land of my ancestors. I do not have much time left to spend on this earth!" he concluded. We wished him good luck and with tears in our eyes, we saw him slowly walking back home. Months later the news of his death will come to us without details.

Fleeing toward the province of Kibuye

In the following days, we continue to walk toward the West in order to reach the province of Kibuye. We cross the wet and forested areas of Gitarama before reaching the dry areas of Kibuye. Every day we are among thousands of refugees on the roads, getting up early in the morning and marching kilometers and kilometers all day in the heat.

A month earlier, around June 23, 1994, a safety zone was established between the western provinces of Kibuye, Cyangugu and Gikongoro. This safety zone is established under the French appellation of "Operation Turquoise," which is composed of about 2,500 French soldiers and about 500 soldiers from different African countries. Many theories have been cited on the actions or the true mission of those French troops in Rwanda at that time. Among all those theories I know one thing: this security zone slowed down the progression of the new Kigali Army conquering the rest of the country; which was killing Hutu refugees in its path. As many will understand later, the new army of Kigali has several reasons to conduct its conquest operations as quickly and ruthlessly as possible. One reason is that they want to stop the killings that continue to be perpetrated against the Tutsi population, but also they want to take revenge on the Hutu who committed or are accused of committing killings. The army wants to kill a large number of Hutu refugees before they escape from the country.

Vehicle of "Operation Turquoise"

During the months of June and August, most refugees and displaced people flee toward or into the safe zone to escape the killings. We are part of those refugees. This safety zone allows us to have time to cross the entire region of Kibuye and Cyangugu provinces right at the border with the Democratic Republic of Congo.

Crossing the border toward Congo (DRC)

We are about ten kilometers from the Congo border. We are resting after long days of walking without relief. But we also want to take a little time to observe the course of events in Rwanda before finally deciding to leave the country. We still have a little hope of returning to our homes, but this little hope is dying as we hear what is happening in other parts of the country.

We are on August 19, 1994, two days before the departure of the military mission of "Operation Turquoise" that had established the humanitarian area. Their two-month term comes to an end about a month after the whole country has officially fallen into the hands of the new Tutsi regime. There is little to no hope of returning to our homes. And we cannot stay here any longer because our being alive is mostly because of this Operation Turquoise's safe zone which will end in two days. A race against time is initiated for refugees to leave the country before the departure of the French mission. Between August 18 and 21, thousands and thousands of refugees cross the different borders that Rwanda shares with Burundi in the South and the Congo in the South and Northwest.

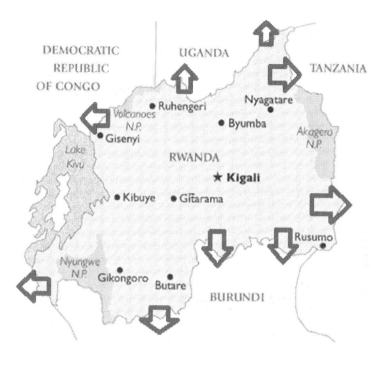

Borders crossed by crowds of Rwandese refugees between April and August 1994

On the evening of the same day of August 19, my family finally decides to leave our country behind. We are sadly walking on the wooden bridge of the *Rusizi* River, one of the small rivers that serve as borders between Rwanda and Congo in the southern part of Lake Kivu. Once we reach the other side of the bank, we breathe sighs of relief thinking that maybe we will finally live in peace without knowing that in a foreign country no one can feel completely at peace. One cannot feel as safe as in one's own country. But at least we know now that there is a border, no matter how small it is, between us and those who want to end our lives. We plan to stay close to our country for some time and hopefully return home soon. We hope that what we are enduring is only temporary.

After having crossed the border to the Congo, we arrive in the city of Bukavu, right on the shore of the southern part of Lake Kivu. This small town, one of the important cities in eastern Congo, has a population of between four hundred thousand and one million when the first Rwandese refugees start arriving between April and July 1994.

Part of the town of Bukavu in Congo

The town is already saturated with thousands of Rwandese refugees sitting in every corner of the city. Local police try to control the flood of refugees who are scattered in the city by moving them away from the center. We are required to go into a nearby temporary camp where all refugees arriving from Rwanda are directed to spend their first night. On their second day, refugees are taken into refugee camps recently opened in the surrounding regions or provinces. In fact, more than ten refugee camps have been opened around the city of Bukavu and in localities within a radius of about fifty kilometers.

That same evening, we are informed that the next day, the UNHCR (UN High Commissioner for Refugees) in accordance with local Congolese authorities will take us to the Inera Refugee Camp located about thirty kilometers away.

Our first night on foreign soil has been peaceful but short. In the morning, we are awakened by the honking horns of the UNHCR trucks that are getting ready to take us to our final destination, the Inera Refugee Camp.

Refugees climbing in UNHCR vehicles for their transport to the camps

Chapter 7

Inera Refugee Camp
(August 1994 - November 1996)

UNHCR vehicles heading to the camps

After a little over an hour of traveling in the trucks of UNHCR through a green and lush area, we end up at Inera. The camp is partially occupied by refugees who arrived before us. We can already see small residential camping huts made of blue and white tarps aligned on a long stretch of ground.

After getting out of the truck, my family and I head to the place for registration of new refugees. After the registration, the UNHCR representative assigns us to someone who accompanies us to the stock supply where we are given a large plastic tarp that we will use to build the hut that will serve as a family home. Some pieces of wood have been prepared for us to use in the construction of the hut. We are given cereals, medicine and other essential things to start a new life with. We are led near other huts and a small plot about four meters by two, delimiting our space, is assigned to us. It is in this latter area that we need to build our "home" where we will live for the next two years! My big brother and I start helping my father to build the hut that will take us a few hours to finish. On the side, my mother and my two sisters are already busy preparing something to eat. Life is beginning! My little brother, who is about two years old, thinks that we are building a house for him to play in.

Refugee camp in constrution

Every hour, trucks unload tens and tens of refugees from the city of Bukavu. The camp is growing every hour. We have new neighbors that we are beginning to get acquainted with. My father starts walking in the neighborhood to inquire about the location of necessary places such as the clinic and toilets.

Two days later, the bush that covered this land has disappeared and we can only see a vast expanse of blue and white tents, each housing a household. Between tents, small passages lead to the clinic, to the stock of food that UNHCR had erected, to the small market in the corner and to the toilets.

New refugee camp

Each day that passes, this small refugee society grows in this camp of Inera. Rich refugees gather to live in one part of the camp and the poor refugees gather in another. The clinic size is growing. Schools are under construction. The market where people buy and exchange goods is growing. Small shops are opening.

Only a few days have passed when a wicked cholera epidemic starts spreading in the camp. Many causes are identified. Sanitary conditions are terrible. The shared toilets which are filling up quickly are located around people's huts and tents. Clean water is lacking. Malnutrition is everywhere because people eat only once a day. And the meal is only corn and beans for most households! People who become ill do not get necessary care or are not treated on time. And people who die are buried near the camp. And the list continues. The Red Cross, Doctors Without Borders and other organizations are struggling to save lives, but they can do little. By the time the epidemic is contained, days later, it will have taken away hundreds and hundreds of men, women and children leaving behind countless widows and orphans in mourning.

Ravages of Cholera epidemic

A large area, just minutes from the camp is opened to bury the dead. To save space, bodies are buried side by side. When someone dies, the family, friends or neighbors carry the body for burial as soon as possible and return to care for those who are still alive. People do not even have time to commemorate the funerals of their relatives who are passing away.

Medical center or clinic in refugee camp

Months pass. My brother, my sister and I register for a school that recently opened to educate children and young people most of whom have already begun to spend their days wandering in the camp or in the market, stealing everything they can lay their hands on. People who know their way around are already beginning to create activities in order to earn their living while the lazy and idle ones spend their time creating problems and disputes with their neighbors over the corn and bean kernels provided by UNHCR. Children are being born while others are dying of malnutrition, lack of hygiene and poor living conditions. There is nothing interesting to do for most people in this refugee camp.

Even the food has no taste anymore because salt and sugar are too expensive. No electricity, television or phone. During the school holidays, the young people and I walk more than ten kilometers early in the morning to buy sugar cane in plantations or farms of local Congolese people. We often come back in the afternoon to resell the sugar cane in the refugee camp and generate a profit that helps me to buy soap, sugar or salt for the family.

Refugee camp in full activity

In the afternoons, I often play soccer with the other young people or we learn and practice gymnastics. There are lots of sporting activities in the camp to keep people busy throughout the day. There is nothing else to do. We have volleyball, football and basketball teams playing each other to pass the time.

Non Government Organizations estimate that more than three million

Rwandese refugees fled Rwanda from April 1994. The DRC itself has received around two million of them, Tanzania received a little more than half a million and Burundi received nearly half a million. The rest is dispersed in Uganda, Kenya and other countries. Most of these refugees have settled in refugee camps while the more fortunate went to live in cities where they melted into the local population.

During these two long years we spend in the refugee camp of Inera, many events take place in Rwanda and in Congo, our country of exile. In Rwanda, life is restarting with difficulties. While some people are celebrating victory, others are bandaging wounds, crying, counting and burying the dead. Farmers are turning over the bloodied soil. People are rebuilding. In the refugee camps, we spend a lot of time listening to the local and international news radio which continues to talk about the recent events in Rwanda. Especially the Radio "Hirondelle" gives us news of Rwanda. It is locally set up by the United Nations shortly after the arrival of Rwandese refugees in Congo. We learn that in Rwanda the new authorities are asking for international assistance to rebuild the mourning nation which is exposed to famine and harbors fear of tomorrow. New authorities are inviting those who have fled to return to the country which, according to them, is now at peace. But few people believe that. This new regime is inviting refugees to return in the country just to make the world believe that everything is fine in the country. But in reality, things are worst that many people think. The news reaching us, brought by people who continue to flee the country, tell us how many Hutus--blamed for the recent Tutsi genocide--are currently being executed throughout the country. Hutu-owned properties are illegally being seized by the military or the authorities of the new regime that often kill or imprison the owners to avoid reprisals. Many Hutus remaining in the country are unjustly imprisoned, simply because they belong to the Hutu ethnic group that is accused of being "responsible" for the genocide.

For our host country Congo, events are quickly unraveling in disfavor of Rwandese refugees! We are at the beginning of the long and contagious Great Lakes region conflict that will engulf the region and will extend over a period of almost two decades. The presence of Rwandese refugees in the eastern part of the country (Congo) is said to be the origin of conflicts between or with some local communities who might be originally from Rwanda or might have distant links with Rwanda. This results in more dramatic and political consequences. One of these consequences is the intention of the Congolese government to repatriate all Rwandese refugees.

In August 1995, the Congolese government, in the person of the Prime Minister of that time, Kengo Wa Dondo, decides that Rwandese refugees must return to their country. Only a few refugees return. A forced repatriation is then considered. We are informed of an ultimatum. After December 31st refugees will be shipped by force back to Rwanda.

As that date approaches, fear spreads. On the night of December 31st the refugee camp is still as full of refugees as it was on the first day. We only have one thing in our minds: tomorrow, trucks will come to pick us up and bring us back in Rwanda by force. We are already imagining how things will unfold. We are already thinking about our probable sad fate once we arrive in Rwanda. Will we all be killed? Imprisoned? Poisoned? We are not going to sit and wait for that moment! We have to do something! We are about halfway through the night: almost half of the refugees in the camp take refuge in the bushes and forest bordering the northern part of the camp. Most of these people are women, children, the elderly and the sick or weak. Men and strong people get up very early that morning and start burning tires and wood in the road, blocking the access of any vehicle to the camp. People do this to prevent trucks from getting into the camp whenever they come to pick up refugees. My family and I spend almost the whole day in the bush. This day marks the first day of 1996! This is a sign that this year will not be a good year for us Rwandese refugees! And finally nothing happens. The trucks do not show up. People who want to repatriate us to Rwanda should be able to see that we refugees like our country, but we do not want to go back home yet. Each person has his/her own reasons that prevent him/her from returning to Rwanda. But some of the common reasons are that people are afraid of being persecuted, expropriated or unjustly imprisoned by the new power. In Kigali, the thirst for revenge is still fresh.

Chapter 8

Destruction of refugee camps
(First Congo War)

Rebels in Eastern Congo

The Alliance of Democratic Forces for the Liberation of Congo-Zaire (ADFL) is a "Congolese" rebel movement that officially starts in South Kivu in late 1996 and is led by Laurent Désiré Kabila. This movement consists of several local and foreign ethnic groups which have different motivations to overthrow or to participate in the war that will overthrow the regime of President Mobutu of Zaire. This movement is directly (or indirectly) supported by Uganda and the Rwandese new regime. I will not go into details on the foundation or the composition of this movement, but I want to say that this movement seems to be determined to destroy all the Rwandese refugee camps in Congo and to massacre all refugees that will escape from the destruction of those camps.

This rebellion of the ADFL, heavily armed, soon begins to operate in the region by inducing terror in the South Kivu region that houses several refugee camps. Refugee camps are violently attacked. Refugees begin fleeing from the camps and the advance of this rebellion.

To ensure the safety of refugee camps, several tens of national military called "Zairian Contingents for the Security of the Camp" had been mobilized and assigned in each refugee camp by the UNHCR.

Toward the end of October 1996, crowds of refugees massively arrive in our camp after walking for hours or days from their camps which were destroyed by the rebels. They arrive in large numbers and tell us about the cruelty of this rebellion. Survivors who escaped from the rebels tell us that many of these rebels speak the Rwandese language and some of them are even wearing Rwandese military uniform. From that moment, many refugees are frightened because they now know that Rwandese soldiers are among these rebels.

One morning in the first days of November 1996, the sun rises sadly as if it already sees a bad day ahead. The faces of refugees emaciated by famine and disease express agitation, fear, confusion, disgust and deep despair. For several days, rumors circulating by word of mouth have been saying that our camp is in the rebels' sights. According to these same rumors, our camp may be attacked at any moment. And those who would attack it may have already taken strategic positions around the camp or are even already inside the camp. We take these rumors seriously because since 1994, ignoring such rumors, many people were badly surprised and dislodged if they were lucky enough not to be killed.

However, this morning we all are prepared for an imminent attack from the rebels. I already know what luggage I will immediately lift and put on my head preparing to run away whenever I hear any detonation or gunshot. My father, my mother and others including neighbors do not take their eyes off their heavy luggage already in front of them. We have agreed to hold each others' hands while fleeing or to keep eyes on the family member in front. We are waiting.

Hearing the silence in the camp and seeing all these frightened refugees, it is clear that we all are waiting for a signal in order to start running, each person in his/her direction with his/her luggage. Scared and traumatized people want to leave the camp while it is still possible. But others don't want to leave the camp before hearing the first shot announcing that the rebels are really there. The soldiers who were supposed to protect our camp and on whom we counted have probably already prepared their bags if they aren't already gone. They know that they would not be able to resist if they decide to fight against rebels.

Our ears are erect like a hare's ears sensing danger ahead, to capture the slightest suspicious noise. Our eyes are wide open and bulging and are observing all movements in all directions.

Around nine in the morning, what we have been waiting for arrives. Thunder of heavy weapons, bombs and rockets followed by torrential light gunshots are heard throughout the camp. We have the impression that it is the end of our little world. Everyone grabs his/her bag, puts it on their head and takes the path that seems best to escape. The first target of rebels is the part of the camp inhabited by leaders, other dignitaries and rich people. There is a stampede around and in the camp. People are running and screaming in all directions. Children are crying. Columns of people are leaving the camp in a hurry, disappearing into the bush. The camp is quickly emptied. There are dead and wounded bodies everywhere. The tarps that constituted our homes are in flames. Old, sick, weak and disabled people who can't move remain in the camp waiting for their uncertain fate.

The camp is in ruins

I am running with a bag on my head. When the attack started, I remember grabbing my bag and starting to run. I do not even remember how and when I got separated from my family members. I keep running among others, getting away from the camp where explosions and gun fire are still intense.

People are fleeing in groups and in different directions. While some of them are taking the direction to the National Kahuzi-Biega Park, others are climbing hills, running on roads and crossing valleys without knowing where they are going.

Destroyed refugee camp

About an hour later, someone who knew my family tells me that he just passed my mother and my siblings looking for me. I decide to sit on the side of the road and wait for them. From a far distance, I see my mother in the middle of a crowd followed by my brother and two sisters. My father and brother are not there. As we continue to walk together, we ask several people if they have seen my brother and father, but nobody seems to have seen them. We continue to hear heavy gun fire and explosions behind us.

In their attempt to take over the Kavumu Airport, located a few kilometers from our camp, the rebels face a small resistance of fighters who are protecting that airdrome. The fights between these two sides last a couple of hours allowing us refugees to flee.

After walking several tens of kilometers towards the north of the country, we decide to stop when it grows dark. We have just started a new march and we don't know where it will lead.

The next day, the march continues until the evening. During the day, as my mother and siblings and I are taking a break to eat the provisions of food that we have brought from the camp, we see my father coming to join us. We are delighted he found us. He begins to tell us how different people told him where and when they saw us, helping him to follow our trail. We did not find my brother whom we believe is not far from us because some people tell us that they have seen him on another path parallel to ours.

Chapter 9

Beginning of a new, long march

The next day, we continue walking north for several hours on the road along the shores of Lake Kivu towards the city of Goma. We finally reach a place called Nyabibwe, located about two hundred kilometers north of the city of Bukavu. We cannot continue on this road because rebels are waiting ahead.

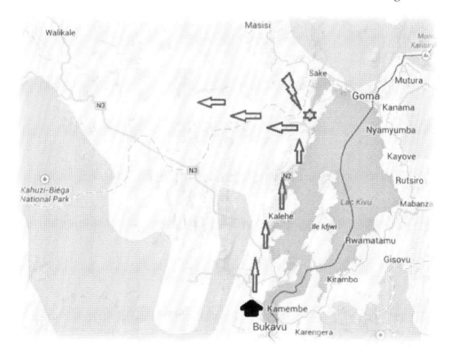

Marching toward Goma

We begin to explore other options. The road we are currently following in order to reach Goma is the only main road in the region. The other road that could lead us to Kisangani--in the North and the center of the country--is tens of kilometers behind us. The time is short and rebels are advancing toward us from both directions. We have to make a decision. The only solution is to abandon this main road and go west through the hills and mountains of the Masisi region. To avoid other surprises from rebels, we decide to start walking right away.

Hills of Masisi

After leaving this town, we encounter bad, narrow and rocky paths, ascending and descending the slopes of hills and mountains. Those who still have them are obliged to abandon their vehicles, motorcycles and bicycles.

Two or three days later, we reach the locality of Shanje, a region of Masisi, with beautiful green valleys, watered by small streams. This landscape is similar to our home and it reminds us that we are still not far from our country! We decide to camp in this locality for a few days.

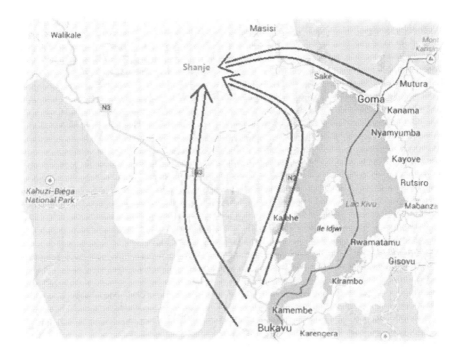

Meeting and gathering of refugees from three different directions

     We are joined by thousands and thousands of refugees. The largest group of refugees arrives from Goma, another major North Kivu town that housed hundreds and hundreds of thousands of refugees scattered in several camps. This region of Goma has also been attacked by the rebels, killing thousands of refugees and pushing hundreds of thousands of them on the roads through the Sake Mountains. They wandered for days, enduring their share of miseries and horrors before ending up in this Shanje Valley. Another group of refugees who join us are those who took the direction of the Kahuzi-Biega National Park after the destruction of the Inera and Gashusha Refugee Camps. We find my big brother in that group of refugees after many days of separation.

Temporary camping of Shanje

We remain camped in this area for a long week. We are feeling comfortable, but the rebellion continues to pursue us and conquer the country. We survive in this region on food that local people give us in exchange for the work we are performing on their farms. People in this region are somehow related to Rwanda because they speak our language Kinyarwanda or a similar language. According to historians, these populations may have migrated here or been separated from Rwanda somewhere at the end of the 19th century. At that time they settled here and acquired vast farm lands.

One afternoon, people suddenly start preparing their bags and leaving the region. At this time, we haven't even heard rumors! In my family we do not know yet what is happening. But I'm sure someone has heard something. We begin to wonder whether we should imitate others and leave. We were just beginning to feel comfortable in this place and here we go again! Perhaps we had already forgotten that the rebels who destroyed our camp were still following us!

About one o'clock in the afternoon, my mother begins to worry when she sees crowds of people leaving. She starts to put together our bags and suggests to my father that we leave while it is still possible. My father tries to oppose her, but she is so convincing that he gives up. An hour later, we are on the way with the others. We are following others hoping that they know where they are going. We have hills and hills ahead of us to climb and descend.

Refugees continuing to flee through hills

Since we did not walk in the past seven days, we are rested. Climbing the first hill is not hard at all, but descending is not that easy because we have bags on our heads. We cling to rocks that serve us as stairs. We cling to tall grass so that we do not slide and end up at the bottom of the valley. Those who are unable to go up or down the hills with bags on their heads are obliged to drop the bags in order to use both their hands when clinging to the grass.

Suddenly we hear engine noise! We realize that it's a plane, resembling a tourists' airplane, flying over the area several times.

Chapter 10

Surprise attack
and
final separation with my father and my brother

Two hours later, we have devoured three hills. Exhausted, we decide to rest, catch our breath and eat something. We brought boiled potatoes as provisions. After finding a comfortable spot to rest, we sit down and start eating the potatoes. Each time I remember this image of our sharing potatoes among my family members, seating on the top of this hill, I recall the Bible scene where Jesus and his disciples share the bread before their dispersion. Without knowing it, we are also sharing our last meal together before our dispersion and separation.

We just finished eating when a distraught man came up behind us shouting that he has just seen, at the bottom of the valley, a long line of men dressed in black, advancing towards the top of the hill where we are resting with hundreds of other refugees. Within minutes, the news has spread. People are frightened. Doubts mingle with fears. This news means that we must leave this place immediately. My father, my mother, my brother, my two sisters, my little brother and I do not wait for a second signal to leave.

We are traveling on a narrow path down the hill. Other refugees join us and soon the road is crowded with frightened refugees. Unfortunately, everyone wants to leave at once! We form rows to avoid crowding and disorder and to allow us to move faster. While we believe that traveling this way will allow us to move quicker, it's quite the opposite! With heavy bags on our heads, we are moving at the speed of snails. To our misfortune, my family members and I are not in the same row. This means that we can become separated because the rows travel at different speeds. And it is almost impossible to change rows because of the long bags we are carrying on our heads.

Tight crowds of refugees

A few minutes later, my row seems to be moving faster at first and then slower than the rows where my family members are traveling. At one point, I do not see any member of my family. I start to panic! I try to leave my row and look for them, but people are so close together that I can't stop, retreat, or move either to the left or right. People start getting upset and shouting. Strong people start shoving weak people to make their way through.

Ten minutes later, after walking about twenty feet, the nightmare starts. A rain of grenades, rockets and gunshots are heard. The rows we formed are broken and everyone is running in different directions. Noises of women and children screaming and crying mingle with the sounds of weapons creating an apocalyptic atmosphere. People abandon their bags in order to run and save their lives. Parents abandon their children. Weak people are collapsing. Bullets are flying through the air searching for their victims. Bullets are ruthlessly surprising and catching people who are running like sheep at the approach of a wolf. Everything explodes everywhere. Lifeless bodies are lying everywhere in a bloodbath. Skulls of dead bodies are crushed and bones of dying people are breaking.

I am running without knowing where I am going like a bird flying into a trap. I decide to abandon the bag I am carrying on my head in order to run. I am running over all sorts of abandoned objects, over dead and dying bodies. People don't know which way to flee. There are two groups of people. One group runs toward the enemy. The other group manages to escape. Among the first group people are killed on the spot and others are captured by the rebels, tortured, killed or brought back to Rwanda by force. I will always remember this 21st day of the 11th month of the year 1996 when this happened.

Later in the evening, I luckily find my mother, my two sisters and my little brother a few kilometers away from this battle field. My father and my brother are gone. We just got separated for the second time. But this time it's for good. This day will mark a painful tear in my family and we will suffer for a long time. Recently in 2012, I had a chance to again see my father and my older brother, sixteen years after our separation. My mother and my sister have not yet had the opportunity to see them since that painful separation day; it's been more than eighteen years.

After walking more than fifteen kilometers, we assume that we have been able to escape the horrible massacres that have just taken place. As we have not yet been caught by rebels, we can rejoice at having fled in the right direction. Many people found themselves fleeing toward the rebel zone. Many of them were killed on the spot and others were captured and taken back to Rwanda.

While dusk approaches, we continue to walk. Nobody wants to stop. We want to keep walking even during the night in order to get as far as we can from the scene of the tragedy. But this region that we are travelling through is bad for walking at night. There are many swamps, valleys and hills and the night is moonless. So we have no choice but to stop for the night.

Later that night, as we sit around the fire, sad memories of the day come back into our minds. We remember that about an hour before the attack, a plane flew over the area we were crossing, spotting all our movements. Some people said that the plane was looking for ways to rescue us, but many others were convinced that the plane was spying on us. Since that day, we never trusted such planes. Later on, another plane tried twice to fly over the area we were crossing, but it did not come back for the third time after being shot at by some people in the refugee crowd.

Chapter 11

In the Rainforest

Entering the rainforest

After a long night of nightmares, we start marching early in the morning. After crossing a deep swamp with rotten water, we travel a few kilometers before entering a forest so dense that we believe we are entering the Amazon forest. The branches and leaves of the giant trees form a waterproof roof that is almost impenetrable to sun light. The forest extends over several hundred kilometers. In the forest, it is raining almost every day. There are countless streams and moist soil everywhere. The land is covered with a muddy crust ten centimeters thick. The forest is uninhabited and has myriads of long vines intertwined and forming barriers to our movements. This is what awaits us! This set of obstacles will worsen our walk and make it difficult for us to cross the forest.

One thing seems weird about this forest, and it is the only thing we could appreciate about it. We never found one cabin or cottage or trace of ruins during the time we spent crossing this forest. Not even a single man or his footprints. This indicates that the forest is uninhabited or has not been inhabited for many years. We never understood where those taros and cassava tubers scattered in abundance throughout much of the forest came from!

Taros   Cassava tubers

People advanced several hypotheses to explain this fact. The inhabitants of the forest who planted these taro and cassava tubers might have been decimated by diseases caused by Tsetse flies that may have invaded the forest years before our passage. For us refugees, it was like a miracle because we saw those tubers as gifts of nature in these difficult times of our lives. They serve as food throughout the time we spend crossing the forest. The time spent was several days for some refugees and several weeks or months for others.

This forest is the beginning of the great equatorial rainforest covering this region of the country. Days are almost always dark. The sun hardly penetrates the forest. Daily rain makes the forest wet and muddy. We are moving through this forest barefoot on slippery slopes muddy enough to hinder our walk. Swamps and small rivers are more than we expected.

Daily walking in this forest becomes one of the most difficult moments of our long journey. We spend all our days in this green hell. We walk all day from morning until evening and at the end of the day we notice that we only walked about five kilometers!

Deep in forest

My little brother, who is only three years old, has to walk by himself just like others, and walking is difficult even for adults. At one point, the poor kid, exhausted, can't take it anymore. My mother and I help him to keep trying but instead of moving forward, he rolls into the mud and resembles a clay statue. This starts to be a problem for us because my mother, my two sisters, he and I are hardly moving forward. I don't know how to carry him because I am carrying my bag. As for my sisters, they barely can move themselves. My mother is so exhausted that she doesn't have the strength to carry her bag and the boy. I conclude that it is up to me to do something. My brother can't move and if I don't do something, we will fall behind and risk being lost forever in this jungle, being caught or being killed by the rebels who are after us.

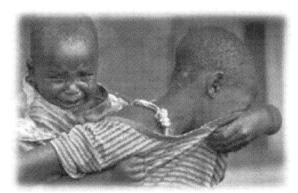

Carrying my little brother

I decide to carry him on my back while carrying my bag on my head, but that is so difficult that I give up. Trying other options, my sisters and I decide to move faster, leaving my mother and my little brother walking slowly behind. After every couple hundred meters, I put my bag down, leave it with my two sisters and go back to carry my little brother on my back. From time to time we alternate and my mother carries the boy on her back while I carry her bag. This approach allows us to move even if we are moving slowly compared to others.

When the evening comes, we start seeking a place to sleep. Usually we stay under a tree which serves as a shelter if it rains during the night. Once we find a good place, we have to prepare the place by removing wild grass. For food, we often look for taros and/or cassava tubers which we will cook.

Fixing cassava tubers to eat

After this meal, often without salt, we lay our bags or clothes on the ground and sleep on them. We spend another night full of nightmares.

Chapter 12

Exit of the rainforest followed by a long painful march

After about a month that seems like an eternity, we are still in the forest. But hope springs from the horizon when we start seeing rays of sunlight that reach us through the huge leafy branches. The forest is getting less and less dense. This means that we are approaching the exit of the forest we believed to be endless. We can see sad smiles that are full of hope. Everyone promises him or herself to spend a month resting once we are out of the forest.

It is about ten o'clock in the morning on a sunny day when we pass a bridge covering clear water flowing over dark rocks. This small river marks the boundary of this horrible part of the rainforest. Each person who comes out of this forest is happy to get out alive.

Traveling with us are two young people who have just abandoned their elderly mother because she was tired and could not move anymore. She was the one who had sadly begged them to leave her there in the forest and continue their way in order to save their own lives. If they had stayed with her, they might all have been lost, captured or killed. They made the same hard choice that many other people had to make during this journey.

After we exit the forest, we are told that rebels might have bypassed the forest to wait for refugees a few kilometers ahead. We want to stop for a while, but people around are saying that it is not safe to dwell here. According to those who have maps and who know how to read them, we must at least walk thirty kilometers a day in order to make up the time we lost in the forest. We are warned that rebels are still after us. And that clearly means that we must hurry to avoid being surprised. We start hitting the road again.

As my mother, my sisters, my little brother and I are moving slowly compared to others, we have to start walking early in the morning around five o'clock. Hours later, around noon, we take a short break of about half an hour to eat something if we are lucky to have it. Then, we resume the march that goes on until about six or seven in the evening, at sunset. We don't try to match the walking pace of other refugees. Despite our efforts we are barely making thirty kilometers a day, while some are making sixty or even more kilometers per day.

Long march

This becomes our daily routine. At sunrise, we pack our bags and start walking before the others. Later in the day, these people we left behind pass us. To catch up with them, my family and I have to walk an hour longer in the evening.

It is difficult to find food to eat. Sometimes along the way, we come across a cassava tubers field or farm abandoned by the local population. We dig deep into the earth hoping to find a few crumbs of cassava tubers to eat.

We are happy to get out of the wet and rainy forest which had miraculous food for us, but now we're on a hot road without food. A hot sun has taken over. We are in the hottest month of the year. The rainy season is over. The sun starts early in the morning and burns all day without interruption until six in the evening. We have our eyes glued on the sky to see if there is at least a tiny cloud bringing rain, but there is nothing. Weeks go by and we are still walking on the road.

One sad day, my little brother becomes very tired from walking. He cannot endure hunger like the rest of us can. In addition to fatigue and hunger, he becomes ill and it is difficult to obtain even one single tablet for fever. Without care and necessary food, my poor little brother loses weight. He weakens every hour that passes and gives up his last breath. Without wasting time, with great sorrow, my mother wraps the little cold and lifeless body in a towel. She brings him to the bush not far from the edge of the road. Someone helps her dig a little pit where she lets him rest. She covers him with a handful of dusty soil and returns to us. We resume the walk. Whatever the degree of our sorrow is, we know that the death of my little brother added a weight on our souls but just removed a weight from our bodies. My family is henceforth reduced to four people: my mother, my twin sister, my little sister and me. We continue walking for several days.

One day, walking in the crowd, I notice a solitary walker, barely moving. Seeing me carrying a heavy bag on my head, the man asks me, "Little brother, until when are we going to run? What is our destination? Months pass, we walk and we keep walking without knowing where we are going! How to find at least the courage to move forward?" Not knowing what good answer to give him, I tell him that I do not know. I only follow others in order to escape death and that's it. His thin face expresses sadness and he continues his plodding and hopeless walk.

In the three months since we left the refugee camps, we have walked almost half of this great country: Democratic Republic of Congo which is the second largest African country.

Toward Nord-West

Chapter 13

The burning road

A sun able to melt the brain is burning from six in morning, heating the long gravel road that runs through the region we are traversing. This is the main road in the region and the only one we can use for our trek. The road is bounded on each side by either a forest or by hostile bush. This road was still under construction when the arrival of the rebellion probably interrupted the final task, placing tar. It is on this unpaved road and on its sun-heated gravel that we are going to spend long days walking barefoot.

Road we are marching on everyday

Days always end badly. Our feet swell as if they hoard water from the hot gravel. The rare shoes that people have carried so far wear out and are of no use. Shoes wear out quickly on this road. Every morning before starting our walk, we wrap old clothes around our feet in order to avoid pain and swelling of the feet. Until this moment, we have traveled barefoot in forests, scrublands, wetlands and swamps without encountering such difficulties and pains! This road is not favorable to us in this daily ordeal.

Our feet without shoes

Usually, the first hours of the day go well. Then, the clothes we wrapped around our feet start to wear out. By the afternoon, we only have tattered clothes on our feet. Then, we need to wrap our feet in new ones. If we don't have anything, then we have to continue walking without protection on our feet. This stage of our journey is disastrous. Men, women and children drag swollen feet on a hot, gravel road. We are walking as octogenarians, burdened with age and awaiting their last hours. Some of us walk with sticks supporting us as we try to put less pressure on our swollen feet.

Walking on the burning road

One day, the sun is warmer than usual. The temperature in the equatorial region during this time of the year rises to forty degrees Celsius (105 degree Fahrenheit). After walking all day without resting, I am very tired and very hungry for the first time. My feet are so swollen and on fire that I can barely take a step.

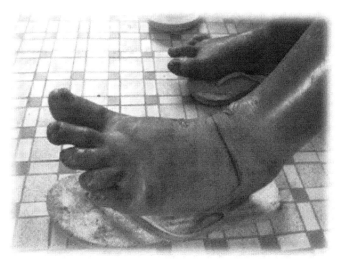

Swollen foot

Every step that I take makes me feel like I am walking on hot coals. It is about six in the evening. The sun has set and we are looking for a place to put our bags and spend the night. We eventually find an unoccupied corner for me, my mother and my two sisters. A soldier among refugees shouts something to all who are camping in this place. He advises whoever wants to live not to spend the night at this place. It is not safe, he says; the rebels are not far away and they might suddenly emerge from an intersection about a kilometer ahead.

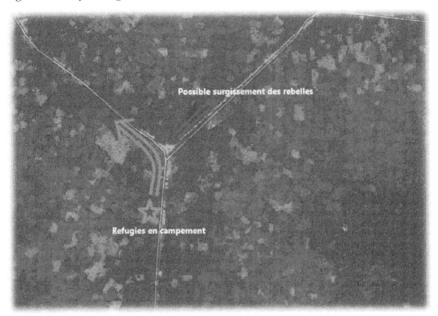

Possible surgissement des rebelles

Refugies en campement

Straight arrow: possible emergence of rebels
Star and arrow: refugees camping and in movement

And in such a case, it would be the end of our misery. But even if life is hard, we still cling to it! After hearing these words, I moan out of pain, despair and disgust. I do not want to walk anymore. I have had enough. My mother begs me to get up and try. Other refugees who heard these words are packing their bags, leaving and disappearing into the dark night. An old saying comes to mind: rather suffer than die. I decide to suffer rather than to die, at least for today!

Ten minutes later, we are walking. Because we do not know if the rebels are already in the intersection that the soldier talked about, we must avoid this intersection, but we must also avoid the main road because the rebels can follow us there with vehicles as they have always done. We decide to make our way through the bush, trying to walk parallel to the main road. The moon and the stars have disappeared under thick, dark clouds covering the sky and making the night as black as coal. We have difficulty walking in this dark, silent and haunting night. We are hustling while we are trying to walk as quietly as possible. It is so dark that we are falling into ditches, bumping against rocks, roots, tree trunks and dead branches. We do not feel pain anymore. We are driven by fear. Often fear or danger makes the body insensitive to pain.

People from the same family try to walk holding hands so that they do not get separated because we can barely see two meters ahead. Unfortunately, others are separated and some of them spend the night calling by name the members of their families to see if they will respond.

After more than two hours of walking, we pass five kilometers beyond the point at which we thought the rebels could attack. We then decide to stop and spend the night. We are in the middle of a scrubland since we want to stay away from the main road. We are vulnerable to wildlife in the bush. It will not take long to see that nature is also against us. We barely lay our heads down when we hear people screaming, jumping and running in all directions at the other end of the camp. We do not understand yet what is happening! Some of us think that rebels found us and are killing people. But a few minutes later we understand that we settled unknowingly on or in a nest of red ants!

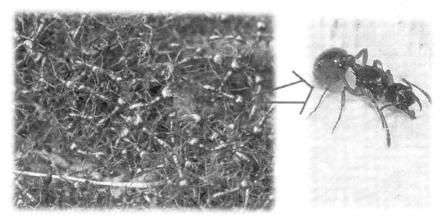

Hostile red ants

We cannot see where these ants are coming from since it is dark. We do not know in what direction to run. They seem to be attacking us from everywhere. They are already getting in our tattered clothes and are biting us everywhere. People strip off their clothes. We remain standing for awhile to allow the ants to calm down.

Chapter 14

Region of Tingi Tingi

The next morning, the march continues despite the soreness of our bodies from the overnight walking and ants' bites. As we travel along, local populations flee their homes thinking that we are the cruel rebels they have heard about. Some of them take refuge in nearby forests where they will stay for a few days; they will not return until after our passage. These local populations who are fleeing at our approach are the ones that should guide us through these unknown regions. Most of us do not have a map of the regions we are traversing. Only the sunrise and sunset help us estimate where east, west, north or south lies. Several times we got up early in the morning and decided, as usual, to walk at least forty kilometers before sunset. We traveled throughout the day and we realized in the evening that we have been walking in a circle. We came back to the same place we left in the morning. This tremendously discouraged us to the point that some of us got tired and decided to just stay and wait for whatever would come.

We have no sense of time anymore. We are just walking. Weeks pass and many of us do not even know what day, week or month it is.

We finally reach the region of Tingi Tingi located in the center of the country. Refugees decide to camp in this region. Perhaps the first refugees decide to camp here because there is a small airfield. My family and I decide to stay here like everyone else. Every day that passes, refugees who had stayed behind are arriving one by one or group by group to join us here. Within days, a large refugee camp housing several thousand people has formed.

Refugee camp forming

As has always been the case for us in new refugee camps, a cholera epidemic is triggered by the lack of hygiene, proper nutrition, clean water and a place to bury corpses. The death toll is increasing every hour and every day as we do not have supplies or food. We can't count the bodies anymore! We are afraid that at this rate we will all be dead, and the camp will be empty in just one month if we are not rescued. The camp is full of skeletal people who look like zombies. Those who are not suffering from different diseases are dying of hunger. Food becomes scarce. People start eating anything they find along the way. Other young people and I start spending hours in the forest, eating different kinds of wild fruit. We are ready to eat anything in order to put something in our stomachs. Strong people, driven by hunger, go in groups every morning into the heart of the forest in desperate search of cassava tubers or prey.

Hunting for a prey

Every morning, about thirty brave people wake up early and leave the camp to go in this desperate search of food. In the afternoon, often half of them will return to the camp empty handed. The other half gets lost in the forest or succumbs to arrows from hostile indigenous people hidden in trees. These natives see us as predators and invaders of their space.

Hostile indigenous hidden in bush

With their arrows, it seems like they have vowed to kill all refugees who leave the camp and venture into their jungles. Although people continue to be killed, this does not prevent a new group from leaving the next morning in search of food. This is the only way to survive here, so people are not discouraged. Better to die struggling. Men prefer to die hunting for something to feed their children rather than see them starving and dying of hunger in their arms. Every day people gather early in the morning at the entrance of the forest in order to enter the forest in a large group, hoping to intimidate the hostile indigenous people armed with arrows.

Hostile indigenous armed with arrows

Some groups manage to have at least one weapon per group so that they can defend themselves in case they are attacked. But this strategy does not seem to work well because the indigenous people know their forests better than we do and they hide in trees to observe and destroy their targets. They manage to first get rid of those who have guns and the rest scatter in the jungle where they will be killed one by one.

The High Commissioner for Refugees (UNHCR) knows about thousands and thousands of Rwandese Hutu refugees who disappeared from radar in the jungles; he learns that some of these refugees are gathering in this Tingi Tingi region. It is a good sign for us. Our rescue is on the way. We start seeing food and medicine arriving in aircraft. We have cereal, corn, high nutritive biscuits and different medicines.

Distribution of cereal, corns and beans

Days pass, and the number of refugees arriving in this newly formed camp increases, and the amount of food provided to feed them becomes increasingly insufficient. People continue to die of malnutrition. In order to have access to health care, in this camp, patients must get up very early in morning to go to the medical center where they spend all day in long lines and sometimes they go back home without care and return the next morning day if they live that long. Some of the diseases are so dangerous that when a person starts getting sick in the morning, that person dies by the evening. That is why many people decide to go for medicine before they even get sick!

A long month passes before the drama starts again. We are still in the camp called Tingi Tingi Refugee Camp. Many Rwandese refugees who went through the deep Congo remember it well. During the long month in this camp, we meet with a cousin who is also the godmother of my twin sister. She became separated from her husband months ago and since then, she has been fleeing with her infant. She begs my mother to let my sister stay with her in order to help her with the infant. My mother agrees. She is camped just a few hundred meters from where we are camped.

Chapter 15

Destruction of Ting Tingi Refugee Camp

One morning, frightening rumors spread that the rebels have already taken and surpassed the Oso River, located about twenty kilometers from our camp. This large river was a safety barrier between us refugees and the rebels. We knew that the day rebels cross this river will also be our last day in this camp of Ting Ting where we have just spent a few weeks.

That morning, every hour that passes increases the fear among refugees who begin leaving the camp. Three or four kilometers from the camp, at Rubutu, there is a small river which is a few tens of meters wide. There is a tiny bridge that the crowd of thousands of refugees must cross.

Noticing the pace with which the camp is emptying, my mother, my sister and I decide to pack our bags and leave the camp as soon as possible. The sad part is that at this moment when we are deciding to leave the camp, we are not with my twin sister. She is still with my cousin. Things are happening so fast that we cannot even go look for her where she lives and we are not even sure if she and her godmother are still there or if they have already left the camp before us.

We decide to leave, hoping to meet them on the way. On the bank of the small river, which has that tiny bridge, are gathered a multitude of people waiting to pass on the narrow bridge. We are wondering how many days it will take for all these people to cross the bridge!

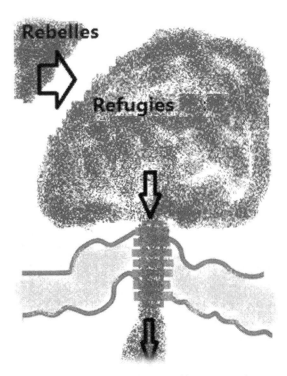

Armed rebels (left) who are after refugees waiting to cross the narrow bridge

My mother, sister and I are among the "weak people" who cannot even try to cross ahead of the strong people or fellows who have guns because they naturally have priority in this situation! It is the law of the jungle out here. The every-man-for-himself situation begins. It is obvious that we (the weak) will cross the bridge last. Suddenly, a column of Mobutu (government) soldiers out for themselves, fleeing from rebels, make their way jostling through the crowd of refugees waiting to cross the bridge. They are brandishing their old, rusty guns to threaten whoever will oppose them or stand in their way. These soldiers know that there is no hope for us refugees because they know how well armed the approaching rebels are. They cannot even protect us!

Some people are losing hope of crossing the bridge until the next day. Worried, they begin inspecting the depth of the water in the river to see if there is a possibility of our crossing on foot. Out of the question! The current of water seems strong and the other shore seems to be far away. We are wondering if the sun will set before rebels find us here because we know they are not far off. And there are rumors that rebels are already among us refugees and are waiting for a signal to pull out their weapons and start massacring us, the poor refugees. We have already formed lines. We are advancing a few steps per hour. Finally, we realize that we are approaching the bridge which we can already see ahead. We can already hear water flowing over the rocks under the bridge. Although the bridge is about twenty meters ahead, we know that it may take an hour for us to cross it.

From nine in the morning until afternoon, we're still here, waiting to cross the bridge. The sunset is already approaching. Suddenly, we hear noises behind us and soon we hear explosions. We already understand what is happening! Everyone tries to hurry across the bridge that we think will snap. Hundreds of refugees jostle like tadpoles in a pond. When everyone only wants to save oneself, charity vanishes. A child shoves his father and his mother, a father stomps his own child, a mother forgets her child, a husband forgets his wife and women abandon their husbands. Weak people, shoved and trampled, are killed or fall into choppy water that carries them away. Seconds later, the bridge is besieged by an abundant rain of gunshots, preventing refugees from crossing and reaching the other shore. To escape from explosions that are blowing up everywhere, we have no choice but to get into the river and cross it on foot.

Crossing the water on foot

My mother, my sister and I try to stay together holding hands while we start crossing the river on foot. We still have our bags on our heads and we hold them with one hand. The flow of water is so strong that my mother tells me to carry my sister on my back because she is so short that she will be engulfed by water if she tries to cross by walking. My mother stays behind trying to figure out how to follow us. The water rises up to my shoulders. I want to throw away my bag and try to swim with my sister on my back, but I remember that I, unfortunately, do not know how to swim. I realize that the heavy bag that I am carrying on my head and having my sister on my back is weighing me down and making it hard to resist the strong current of the water.

Crossing the river on foot

The current of water eventually carries away many refugees. With my sister on my back, I am fumbling through the water, clinging to rocks. Those who manage to reach the other side of the river are also the targets of gunshots from rebels preventing them from escaping.

In this deafening noise of gunfire and explosions, we are able to reach the other side of the river by the grace of God. After having set foot on dry land, I look behind me to see if my mother is still where we left her. I want to go back and help her if it is possible. But instead of seeing her, I only see smoke from an explosion arising from the place where I remember leaving her. Not seeing my mother anymore, I sadly think that it is over for her!

Many people die in this very place! Only this river that carries their corpses and drinks their blood will know how many of them! Tingi Tingi is one of the memorable places of this great Congo, stained by the blood of the poor Rwandese refugees.

Gunshots and explosions continue to be heard. Rebels are blindly killing the largest number of refugees they can. I tell my sister that we must get rid of all our bags and save our lives. I hasten to open my bag and pull out some milk powder packs and a couple of pieces of soap that my mother had put into it. I decide to throw away the remaining contents of the bag which consisted of old cooking pots, clothes and other things. When my sister finally gets rid of the few things she has, we rush to get on the road where people are running, not believing yet that they made it out alive. Nobody is talking. We can only hear our footsteps on the dusty road. Dust rises around the passing, frightened crowd of refugees.

Running away from the death scene

We barely get past this bloodied scene when we see a helicopter, certainly one of the enemies', flying over our heads. It comes and goes. Every time it approaches our position, we hide under trees. After walking about three kilometers, we end up meeting my mother again. I'm more surprised than pleased because I believed her to be dead.

Three hours later, about twenty kilometers away, the night falls while we are still on the road. But we do not stop until the night gets really dark to the point that we no longer see the road we are walking on.

At night almost everyone is complaining about having been separated from at least one family member and having abandoned the only cooking pot and clothes that remained. Thus, we have been separated with my twin sister. Since then, we have not seen her or heard from her.

Chapter 16

Marching westward, full of rivers

Several days of walking follow. We continue to flee across the country toward the West. We arrive at a river. Only indigenous people live nearby. These people do not know what money is or how to use it. They live all their lives in these dark corners of the world, deep in the forest. They live off fish offered by this river that runs through their little world: the forest. In order for us refugees to cross the river and continue our walk, we offer them goods such as clothes, soap, spoons, plates, matches, etc. They take us in their wooden boats to the other bank of the river.

Crossing the first river on boat

This part of the country has many rivers, and we are able to cross them by offering goods to the local population.

By the time we reach Ubundu, the largest river we have encountered so far, we have nothing left to offer. Besides, there is not even one boatman to offer something to. We are told that authorities on the other side of the river do not want refugees on their land. Because of that, they forbade all paddlers to cross the river and bring refugees. We are stuck here while rebels are still advancing behind us without obstacles. This time, no one even thinks about crossing this river on foot as we did a few weeks ago. Already hundreds of refugees are camped here and the number of refugees arriving is increasing by the hour.

Desperately waiting for a boats

From morning until evening, we are sitting on the shore of the river, desperately searching, the length of the river to see if people on the other side will remember us and let boats come to get us before rebels capture and kill us. Hunger starts to make its massacres among refugees. We constantly ask ourselves why we fled for months and months to end up dying here of hunger or at the hands of rebels whom we escaped several times!

We start regretting that we did not just stay in our country and be killed there instead of dying after enduring all this pain.

The wait continues. Desperation is growing. Fear begins to stimulate imaginations and creativities. We need to cross this monstrous river. And for us to cross it, we need canoes, boats or things that look or have the same functions as boats. People who have strength, resources and knowledge start cutting down pieces of bamboo and making rafts that are shaped like canoes.

Bamboo handmade raft

Right next to us, a small family of four is working on one of those bamboo rafts. After cutting a couple pieces of dry bamboo, they line up the pieces and tie them together tightly with strings. At the end, they inspect their work and conclude that everything is in order. They slide the raft in the water and the raft starts floating as expected. Many people who have followed step by step the making of this raft have already attacked the small forest of bamboo which is right behind the camp planning to make their own rafts. The four members of this family jump on the raft with their bags, sad smiles on their faces. A crowd of spectators has already gathered around. "When we get to the other side of the river, we will beg the authorities to let boatmen come look for all of you," said the oldest member of the family to the crowd. As oars, they dip their hands in the dark water and start rowing toward the other side. They row in a straight line and in a direction that is perpendicular to the water's flow. At first, everything seems to go perfectly. Suddenly, when they arrive almost in the middle of the river, everything changes. The strong current begins to divert them. They use all their strength to control the raft. But they run out of energy. They cannot withstand the strong current that is already carrying them away. Without any rescue, the river silently carries them away. We see them desperately wave their hands seeking help, but we can do nothing. At least they will die bravely trying to save themselves. The water carries them to a deep fall like an abyss and there, they disappear from our sight. We can do nothing; it is their destiny!

Approximately two long weeks go by and we are still desperately waiting. It is often said that it is sometimes in despair that the little light of destiny appears at the horizon. According to rumors, we are all convinced that rebels will arrive in this camp today. No one is talking; we all are desperate and frightened.

It is late in the morning. The fog still envelops the Ubundu River. From a distance, we see a few large boats leaving the other shore coming in our direction.

Boats finally arriving

Minutes after seeing the boats, we start packing our bags. Everyone rushes to the shore where these boats will stop. In about half an hour, almost the whole camp is at the shore ready to go. Hope finally returns. "God has heard our prayers," say many rejoicing refugees. Before the boatmen even cast anchors to tie their boats, people are rushing and jumping into the boats. "Hundred dollars per person," shout the boatmen. "Valuable goods or items are welcome; we are in a hurry," they add. My mother, sister and I have none of these things. Goods! We only have an old pot blackened by smoke and the tattered clothes that we are wearing. Money! It's not even worth talking about it. Now it has been about a year since we even touched a single bill. We are sad and perplexed when contemplating scenes where people are offering boatmen different types of things including clothes, suits, jackets, and bicycles--for those who still have them--shoes, plates, pots and even spoons. We are wondering what miracle we will have to perform in order to cross this river. We are hopeless.

In front of us a large family just rented a boat and they are preparing to occupy it. With a sudden gesture, my mother takes our hands, me and my sister, and without even a word to the boatmen or to the renters of the boat, we sneak into the boat in the same time other people are getting in with their bags.

Noticing our intrusion, a boatman asks my mother for money:

"Lady, where is the money?"

"I do not even have a penny on me," answers my mother. In a threatening tone, the boatman advises us to get out of the boat before he throws us into the river. My mother begs him to have mercy on us, but his tone and threats make us believe he will overturn the boat because of us three. To appease his rage mother finally asks him:

"How much in total?"

"Three hundred dollars."

"Okay."

My mother points to a nice suitcase that is not even hers. Many people are crammed together with their bags on top of the nice suitcase. My mother tells the man:

"Please, could you get me that suitcase right there? This is where I hide the little money I have left."

"How? We cannot tell all those people to stand up! We are in a hurry! You will pay me when we get to the other side of the river!"

"That is perfectly okay; just remind me," replies my mother.

The boatman returns to his other clients. His teammate is busy collecting money and all kinds of goods in a small bag. We are already leaving the shore with an inexpressible relief. There are about twenty people with bags on board this long, old boat that rocks due to strong waves raised by the wind.

Crossing Ubundu River

It takes us about twenty long minutes to cross the river, twenty minutes during which the two rowers fight fiercely against the powerful waves and current that threatens to divert and carry away the boat. We are slowly approaching the shore, and we can see other refugees unloading from other boats. Without even waiting for the boat to reach the shore or touch the dry land, my mother, sister and I jump off the boat with our bags and we start running, vanishing into the crowd of refugees. This is how we came to cross this river and escape the boatmen who were asking us for the money we did not have.

About five minutes pass after we cross the river when a heavy storm sweeps through the entire length of the river, raising huge waves. Hundreds of refugees who were still crossing are swallowed by the monstrous river. Their bags go along with them to their final resting place.

Like other refugees, we decide to camp in this locality, a kilometer from the bank of the river, for a few days. We must get ready for a possible, new and long walk. As in every new refugee camp, hunger and disease start wreaking ravages.

Chapter 17

"Hitamo!" which means "Choose! »

The only road out of the camp divides after a kilometer into two roads leading to two different destinations. For all refugees that are camped here, deciding which route to take becomes a dilemma, and that is why refugees call this place "Hitamo!" which means, "Choose!" in the Rwandese language.

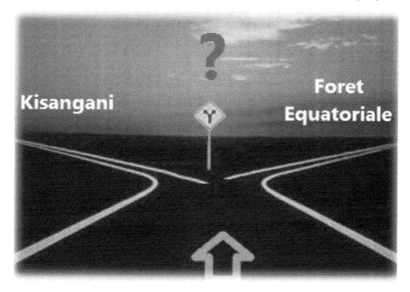

Kisangani OR Forest

Refugees spend days thinking about which is the best road to take. We have to choose the road entering the rainforest or the one leading into the region of Kisangani. Certainly the two roads do not lead to Rome! People are saying that the first road sinks into the rainforest where there are different kinds of wild animals, tsetse fly swarms, poisonous snakes and many other dangers. The long forest road is uninhabited, dark, has many rivers, has nothing to eat, etc. According to how people are describing it, it is worse than hell. This discourages those who are thinking of taking this road. Perhaps the other road is better. It is large, spacious, shorter, surrounded by houses, trees and gardens. The bad news is that this road leads to Kisangani, a large city already conquered by Kabila's rebels who have been killing refugees and pursuing us for months. Those who prefer this path should expect three outcomes unless destiny decides otherwise. They will be killed on the spot, tortured to death or be repatriated by force to Rwanda for an uncertain fate. That thought seems even worse than going into the forest. Those who think that going to Kisangani is the best choice discourage those who want to take the other road going into the forest. Those planning on entering the forest regret the fate of those who want to go to Kisangani. Indeed, the road through the forest is used to bypass the city of Kisangani already taken by the rebels.

A small family comes to my mother asking her what choice she made. "I do not know yet, I have not decided yet," replies my mother. The forest! And what if it is like the one we went through a few months ago, or worse? Maybe we will not get out of this one alive. Going to Kisangani? No! We have not walked hundreds and hundreds of kilometers, suffering throughout those regions, forests and rivers to give up now by surrendering to the clutches of rebels.

While some refugees make decisions, others are confused and do not know what to do. They decide to stay here in the camp, but this is not a good solution either because rebels will eventually arrive here by the road from Kisangani or by the river which is a kilometer away. So it is just a matter of a few more days.

After about a week of thinking, fear of the imminent arrival of rebels spreads through the camp causing refugees to make their final decisions. Refugees are already starting to withdraw one by one. Everyone, listening to his heart, conscience or instinct has made a choice: Kisangani, forest or staying. A woman my mother knows from back in the country takes the road toward Kisangani. A few months later, we learn that she and her family members were brought back in Rwanda. My mother finally makes the decision that we will enter the forest. This is what her instinct advised her. May God help us!

It is about five in the evening. The sun is already setting. We are silently making our way through giant grass that covers the small path where we are walking toward the equatorial forest. Thick tree branches deprive us of the last sunlight. We do not know when or if we will see sunlight again.

We have walked a couple of kilometers when a dark cloud covers the region announcing the night. We decide to stop here for the night.

The next day at dawn, we start walking through the forest. We are surprised that this forest is not as terrible as it was described to us. The forest is not that dense. We were told that we will encounter many rivers that we will not be able to cross. But it is rather the opposite. Water becomes so rare at one point that we spend several days without washing. It is a problem to find water to make food and it is difficult to find pure water to refresh our dry throats.

We have been walking for two days without finding even a drop of water. It is terrifying. Even the little water that often stagnates in the hollow of the road or in marshes has evaporated due to the hot Ecuador sun that ravages this region. Dehydrated, our bodies begin to weaken. Miraculously, on the way, we see a small puddle of water in the roots and in the shade of a big tree. That small puddle has resisted the intense heat.

Collecting rare water

This water has turned almost black, and it has attracted mosquitoes that came to find shelter from the ravages of the heat. After discarding those stubborn mosquitoes, we collect the water for drinking and cooking food. We do not even have time to think of the health consequences of using this water because we have no choice!

Chapter 18

Detour by Ikela

As the west region of the country has many rivers including the great Congo River, we decide to change directions to avoid that region.

Avoiding Kisangani

We start walking toward the South, where two small towns, Boende and Ikela, are located. When we arrive at the junction of the two roads that go to the two towns, we decide to take the one going toward Boende. After walking nearly ten kilometers, the local population informs us that the town of Boende has recently been conquered by rebels. Surprised and frightened, we ask them if there is a different way, and they advise us to go back to the intersection and take the other road. We immediately turn around and head back to the intersection and take the road going to Ikela, a small town located a few tens of kilometers across the town of Boende.

This town of Ikela is a gathering place for many soldiers of the Mobutu government and their families. They have fled areas already conquered by the rebellion.

Congolese soldiers fleeing with their families

The presence of these soldiers is perhaps the reason why the city has not yet been conquered or attacked by rebels. We know it will not be long before the city is attacked by rebels who are in the neighboring town of Boende. For that reason, we must hurry to cross this region. We are currently looking for a path that will lead us to the western town of Mbandaka.

My mother, sister and I are alone and slowly moving toward the entrance of the little town of Ikela. From a distance, we see a small group of people sitting on their bags. They are refugees. We immediately think that they are tired and are recuperating and catching their breath before continuing their walk. This is something we often do. After walking two or three hours, we often sit down and take a break for about ten minutes before continuing. Since we are not tired, we continue our slow and monotonous walk without worrying about them because we don't care about how they are managing their walking habits. Noticing our ignorance of what is going on in this little town, these refugees stop us and explain the situation to us.

We learn that these soldiers who found refuge in this small town of Ikela are plundering Rwandese refugees as they pass by. With old guns and some bullets they have left, they terrorize and rob the refugees, leaving them almost as naked as newborns!

Since there is no other way to avoid this town, we must pass through this city at all costs. Therefore, we need a strategy or a plan to go through without being stripped of the little goods we have left. For my little family, we have no fear of being robbed because we have nothing important anyway. But we are afraid that if they do not find anything to take from us, they may harm us. We also learn that these soldiers tend to rob small lonely groups of refugees. The plan is to wait for other refugees in order to form a large group before entering the town. Our hope is that the robbers will be afraid to attack a large group.

We join the group and wait for other refugees who are arriving one by one or family by family. They do not know about the situation. Half an hour later there are about sixty refugees in the group. One or two people must stay behind to inform other refugees of the situation as they come after us. This person will leave with the next group which will also leave behind one or two people and so on.

Before we start walking to enter the town, we agree not to panic or back down if the robbers try to intimidate us. We have to keep moving forward. We agree to walk and stay in a group. No one should stay behind or walk ahead of the group. Each group of refugees makes sure it has among them someone with a gun that walks in front of or beside the group.

Group of refugees

In our group, there is one refugee who happens to have a gun. He decides to walk beside us. Used to a slow but steady walk, my mother, sister and I adapt to the walking pace of this group that consists mainly of men and strong people. We are doing our best since we cannot afford to stay behind.

We are silently walking, our bags on our heads, clinging to others to be at least among the last people of the group. I want to cough, but fear prevents me. After walking about half a kilometer, roofs of houses start appearing telling us that we are entering the town. We walk as fast as we can through the city. All is silent. It looks like an abandoned city, ravaged by war. Happy birds are singing in the tree branches on this day which is beautiful despite the scorching heat.

Ahead we can see the small town's limits. The fear begins to leave us as if the danger is already passed. The road becomes narrower and the surrounding bush starts to appear. Suddenly, we hear something moving through the giant grass on both sides of the narrow road. About ten soldiers emerge from both sides of the road with hair and eyes like drug addicts. They block our path, aiming their old, rusty guns at us. In Lingala dialect, they scream and yell, telling us to drop our bags and run. For about a minute, none of us has the courage to move forward while the robbers continue to hoarsely convince us to put our bags on the ground. Fearing to stay behind, I find myself in front of the group. If these brigands shoot us, I will be the first victim. Seeing their guns pointed at us with their weapons, I am already thinking about the end of my miserable life on this earth. We make a hesitant first step, then the second. Seeing that we are not giving up, they adjust their guns to warn us that another gesture will cause them to spray us with bullets. We have the strength to resist because we know that these soldiers do not kill innocent or unarmed people just like that. Unable to maintain their patience any longer, some of them start shooting in the air, over our heads, in order to scare us. One of them fires a bullet that digs a small hole a few inches from my toes. I almost drop my bag and run into the bush which is on my right. They are still positioned about twenty meters ahead. They are surprised that other than a thrill that grips us, the twenty or more bullets they shot in the air did not frighten us as they hoped. We make one, two and three more steps forward. They take the same number of steps backward. I am really not afraid to drop my bag because I know that there is nothing good in it except the supply of a few rotten cassava tubers. The only fear I have is that they will take my life which I have not lost in other times as tough as this. Losing their patience, the furious robbers start shooting in the air again to disperse us, but we are determined not to move unless we are moving forward. Out of bullets, they are surprised to see a man emerging from among us. He challenges them shooting into the air. Not expecting this at all, they scatter back into the bush like rats at the sight of a cat. Without wasting a second, we resume walking and about five minutes later we are out of the town and entering a small forest. That is how we passed through the town of Ikela and got to keep our bags and saved our lives.

Chapter 19

Marching toward Mbandaka

After leaving the town of Ikela, we continue walking for about two days, detouring around the town of Boende. We avoid it since it is already under the control of rebels. When we come back on the main road, tens of kilometers beyond the town of Boende, we continue walking west to Mbandaka.

New destination

Our long and painful walk eventually leads us to a small locality, about ten kilometers from the town of Mbandaka, one of the biggest cities in the province of Ecuador, northwest of the country. At the entrance to this place called Wendji Secli, a barrier is erected with more than a dozen of old Mobutu's soldiers disarming all soldiers or armed people among the crowd of refugees arriving every day. Over-using their authority, these soldiers, weakened by hunger, the warm climate and old age, spend their days stripping refugees of money and the few remaining assets they were able to keep until now. They are taking anything that can be of value. And apparently they have the authority to search the bags and the clothes we are wearing. Refugees who still have money find themselves dispossessed. Some women take their money and that of their husbands, put it in their hair and braid on top of it. This is the only place where many of those soldiers did not think to look. Those who are honest among the soldiers confess later that the arrival of Rwandese refugees enriched them.

We decide to settle in this locality for a few days. Refugees are arriving from different directions and are joining us. Hunger, thirst and diseases start taking their toll. Tens and tens of refugees are dying every day. Some of their bodies are disposed of in the river nearby. Whenever we feel weak and hungry, we swim and drink water from the same river in order to regain strength. The few measures of corn grains that the Red Cross gave us on our arrival day are gone. We do not even know where to go begging for food. Days come and go; people continue to die and the river continues to take away their corpses. The Red Cross, overwhelmed, withdraws and helpless refugees are abandoned to their sad fate. What will be our fate? God alone, who still keeps his hand on some of us, knows.

On the seventh day, we decide to leave this place that is becoming haunted by the dead every day. And we are told that the rebels who have already conquered more than half of the country are in nearby centers getting ready to attack the hundreds and hundreds of refugees gathered here.

The date is May 13, 1997. It is still very early in the morning. We decide to take the road toward Mbandaka because we fear an imminent attack by rebels. We also hear that in Mbandaka there is a boat waiting for Rwandese refugees in order to take them to the neighboring country, Congo Brazzaville (Republic of Congo).

About ten kilometers separate us from the town of Mbandaka. Taking the only road, we begin to devour the ten kilometers. On the road, old vehicles full of people, especially women, pass us going in the opposite direction. They are going to the market at the town we just left because today is Tuesday which is market day. Local residents are leaving their homes and coming to settle along the road watching us pass by.

Walking toward Mbandaka

They are watching this crowd of emaciated, barefoot refugees, badly dressed, carrying heavy bags on their heads. As they walk on the dusty road, they do not have the appearance of human beings. They look like observers of the Tour de France gathering along the road and watching bikers pass. Some of them are making fun of us, but others who see our suffering seem to feel pity for us. To show us their solidarity and compassion, some of them bring buckets full of water and distribute cups of water to refugees who want to refresh their throats. Others hand us mangoes, oranges and bananas. At this point the sudden charity begins to spook us because since we started to cross this country, no other people have done such a thing. The sun has already risen from the horizon and illuminates the area. People are attending their everyday activities. Some of them are drinking their hot coffee along the roadside. Merchants are opening their shops. Beggars are making themselves comfortable in the shadows of trees and in intersections. Thieves are already lurking around shops, examining their future loot. Almost everything is in movement, and this tells us that the city is not far away. Accustomed to spending days, weeks and months in forests or desert regions, we feel like we are entering one of those big African cities.

We have just started the sixth kilometer and we only have four left in order to reach the port of Mbandaka and board a boat that might be waiting for us. Everyone swears not to rest before stepping on that boat that will finally bring us back to life!

Occupying almost the entire width of the road, we are silently moving forward until we are suddenly dispersed by the return of the vehicles that passed us a few minutes earlier going to the market.

Vehicles transporting merchants and goods

Honking, traveling at a crazy speed and raising a dusty cloud, these vehicles pass toward Mbandaka where we are headed. Are they racing? Are they chased? By whom? We conclude that they might be rushing to pick up more customers. But we do not understand why these vehicles came back with the same people they had when they left. We try to focus on our walk.

A few minutes after the passage of these vehicles, we hear rumblings behind us similar to those of thunder. But the sky is blue and there are no clouds announcing rain. We are in the dry season of the year. This is definitely not thunder. A blast of heavy gun fire tells us that rebels have attacked the locality we just left. The drivers had to turn around. This explains why they were driving crazy. Now we know that rebels are only about seven kilometers behind us at the place we just left. Certainly many other refugees were still there!

Fear takes over the hunger that was consuming us. The explosions that we could barely hear a few minutes earlier are increasing as rebels approach. Suddenly, the refugees who were around me, my mother, and my sister double their walking pace and disappear from our sight. We know that rebels are surely coming in vehicles while we refugees are on foot. Our past passes before our eyes and we start thinking that rebels will finally catch us. As usual when the situation gets tough, refugees are beginning to abandon their bags and run to save their lives. I tell my mother that we must hurry to get on the boat which might be waiting for us to take off! After hearing the distant gun shots and explosions, local people who were gathered on the road watching us went back into their homes.

Chapter 20

In the town of Mbandaka

The long road

Several minutes later, we reach the center of Mbandaka. We are at the gate of the port. Almost all buildings have rusted roofs giving the impression of being built during the colonial era.

All of the port gates giving access to boats are locked. Only people who know how to climb and who have strength are climbing the walls and gates of the port to go inside and cram into the boat already crowded with refugees. I do not know how to climb and besides, I do not even have the strength.

Unable to get to the boat, I desperately look through the hinges of gates and I see a crowd of refugees in and around the boat.

Cursed boat

I continue looking to see if the boat will leave, hoping that someone will come in time to open up the port gates so that we can join the boat before it sails. But the boat is not leaving yet. In my heart I am thinking that maybe the ship is waiting for more refugees including me.

Immobile and helpless, my mother, sister and I continue to watch refugees who arrive, climb the wall and go to the other side of the port. Losing hope of getting on the boat, we decide to sit down and rest near the port while we think about what to do. We still know that rebels with their trucks are less than five kilometers away, and they will cover this distance in no time. A Congolese woman in her fifties sees us sitting and resting in front of her house. She feels pity for us and offers us a papaya to eat.

Some residents of Mbandaka who have long followed the progress of the rebels in their country are convinced, after hearing the distant explosions, that today May 13th is the day of liberation of their city by the Kabila soldiers that they have been waiting for. Many Congolese people wanted a change after the rule of Mobutu that lasted more than three decades.

The city seems strangely empty. Everyone has returned to their homes except homeless people and we refugees who still wander the suddenly deserted streets of the city. Mbandaka is a city surrounded by many rivers.

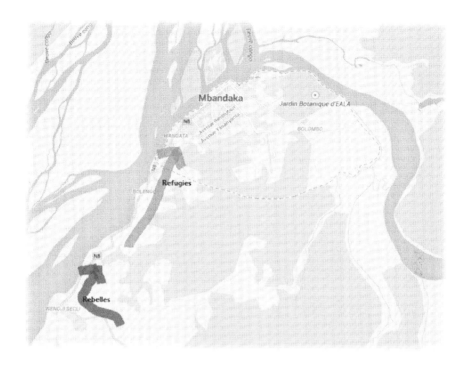

Mbandaka surrounded by water

There is only one road out of this town and that is the road we came through. And it is the same road rebels are coming through. This means that we cannot go back. It is too late. Basically, we have reached our destination. The only way out we can think of is to find small boats and escape by the rivers. Where could we find a boat and a guide since almost everyone is already in their homes? And if by chance we find one, the price will be impossible to pay.

It is around nine in the morning. We have almost finished eating the papaya that the woman gave us. Suddenly, we see people running. For a minute we do not understand. Meanwhile the woman, who was standing on the roadside watching our refugee brothers come and go, comes running toward us. She says: "They are already here; we need to hide." She has barely finished her sentence when a rain of light and heavy gun fire is heard throughout the city. Suddenly, the gate to the port is open and armed rebels make their triumphal entry. They first deal with people crammed into the boat and waiting in vain for their departure. I imagine the surprise and confusion they experience when seeing rebels entering the port. Is it necessary to say what happens next? I am lucky not to be inside the port or on the boat to witness what happens exactly. We are hiding just a few meters away, and following is the testimony of the few survivors who luckily escaped from that boat.

According to survivors, that boat full of humans was an old boat that was abandoned there in the port for weeks or months. People intentionally lied to refugees telling them to get on that boat. Some people even say that it was a plot that had been put in place to attract many refugees into that boat in order to exterminate them in large numbers. Returning to the testimonies, after detaching the anchor of the boat, rebels let the boat go along with the flow of water away from the edge. Then, the rebels fired several rockets at the boat. Almost everyone who was on the boat was killed except a few good swimmers who were able to escape by diving into the water and swimming for several hundreds of meters.

Since many refugees dove into the water to escape, rebels waited for those who would surface planning to put them out of their misery. This river swallowed so many refugees' corpses that later, local residents got angry and complained about not being able to drink or use the water anymore because, they said, the water was spotted by many bodies of Rwandese refugees.

Refugees' corpses in the river

Some of them do not even want to eat fish caught in these waters since they say the fish ate the flesh of corpses and drank their blood.

Those who loved to swim in the river do not swim anymore because they sometimes find themselves swimming beside a floating dead body. A few months after those sad events, walking on the shore of the river, I see young people swimming, playing and shouting, "Tala ebembe ya Rwandais!" This means, "Look at this Rwandese dead body!"

Let's return to the events. After finishing with people in the boat, a hunt for refugees follows in the streets of Mbandaka. Anyone badly dressed who looks like a refugee is killed on the spot. After this blind killing, at least one body of a local resident, a mental patient, was found among corpses of refugees when the city was being cleaned up. That day he was thought to be a refugee because of the way he looked or was dressed.

Gun fire and explosions can still be heard everywhere and we are wondering if all this is to kill people, to intimidate enemies or if there is a military resistance. Bullets are flying at a height of one meter and shooters are looking everywhere to shoot whoever raises his head. My mother, little sister, I and other refugees who are next to us, are crawling in the bush to avoid being struck by the stream of bullets passing by and whistling above our heads. We crawl away from the main road.

We arrive in the shadow of a wall of a house under construction, and we decide to remain hidden while squeezing ourselves against the wall to avoid being spotted. About thirty minutes later, gunshots decrease and finally stop. Rebels think they have killed all the refugees or they are tired of killing refugees. When we raise our heads to look up, we see a tiny building without form made with sheet metal in a backyard, about thirty feet away. We want to hide in there, but we wonder how we will get there without being noticed.

Hidden in a shower place

The only way is to crawl there. But crawling will take us a long time, my mother thinks. Without thinking about another alternative, she runs without wasting time, and three seconds later, she is there. My sister and I follow her. We soon find out that this building is a small shower that gives off a damp smell. It is about three feet square, has no door and is located in a backyard of a house off the main road. Suddenly, we hear heavy steps of soldiers walking behind us through the grass, exchanging words in Swahili. We feel our hearts leaving us. We strive to hold our breath and avoid touching the metal sheet walls. We hear soldiers walking away. They do not look into this shower because perhaps they do not think people can hide in such a place.

We stay in this shower place, standing still, during the rest of the killing that will amount to a large number of deaths in Mbandaka. Months later, private investigators will come to Mbandaka asking about the massacres of Rwandese refugees in this city of Mbandaka, but we will refuse to talk to them for fear of reprisals.

An hour later, gun shots have ceased and the town has become silent. The rebels' mission is complete. We did not hear it with our ears, but we were told later that after the mass killing of refugees, rebels drove through the streets with loudspeakers shouting in Lingala, the local language, that whoever hides a refugee shall die with that refugee and that whoever is kind enough to hide a refugee had better get rid of the person.

Soon these words reach the ears of the owner of the small shower place in which we are hiding. She remembers that earlier at the beginning of the attack, refugees ran toward the backyard of her house. She is certain that some of them are still hidden there. With her son, she comes out in her backyard and there we are! A few minutes later, the entire household is passing by the shower place throwing us scornful, hateful and sometimes pitying glances.

Fearing to die with us, driven perhaps by her household, this old woman comes back and approaches us whispering something in Lingala the local language that we do not understand. Noticing that we did not understand, she starts telling us whatever she wants to tell us. We soon understand that she is asking us to leave. In response, my mother whispers something in French. This woman knows French well! She begins spewing a flood of words to make us understand that we must leave her property before she dies because of us. We pretend to have understood but in truth, not having heard the threats of the rebels, we do not understand what spirits visited this woman convincing her to throw us out. We are only poor refugees, seeking a shelter to hide from the death that is running in the roads of the city. With threats, she starts pulling us out using force, telling us that if we refuse to get out, she will call the soldiers to get rid of us for her. We beg her for mercy, but she is deaf to our tearful supplications. When she suddenly disappears, we think that she is going to bring a weapon or call the soldiers as she just threatened. We then think that it is over for us. We are probably living the last minutes or seconds of our lives on this earth. The hope for mercy and grace in the eyes of this woman disappears. If she pushes us out on the road and rebels see us, the rest will be in God's hands.

After three long minutes, she reappears carrying in her hands three pieces of white fabric with strings. We think that she wants to tie us up. It seems like the short time she spent in her house preparing these strings calmed her rage. Without our asking her a question, she starts to explain to us what is going on. She concludes that these pieces of fabric have meaning: whoever wears them on their forehead, like a banner, manifests joy and supports the rebels who just liberated the town from the dictator. Does she really want us to wear these pieces of fabric on our foreheads to show joy and support to those who chased us, killing refugees all the way from the border of our country! Unfortunately, we have no choice now, but to accept in order to save our lives. Before my mother opens her mouth to ask her questions or request an explanation, the woman has started attaching the banners on our foreheads. She urges us to get out and wishes us good luck. Unable to do anything else, and especially not wanting to put this woman in danger, we accept our fate. We can see sadness looming on her thin face assuring us that this was not her own will. As we move away, she follows us with her eyes wondering what will happen to us.

Chapter 21

Saved by a sentry

We are walking along Avenue du Congo (named Avenue Mobutu in those days). The road is deserted and bordered by a long row of deciduous trees. Besides the soft sound of our bare feet on the asphalt, we cannot even hear a pin dropping. From one end to the other of this avenue, you can see only our three moving silhouettes. The slightest sound of a car engine increases the beating of our hearts. A woman in her thirties emerges from the old buildings on our right and crosses the road. My mother rushes toward her and begs her to hide us. "You have no luck, I am already hiding two refugees in my house," she replies disappearing into the giant grass on the left side of the road. We're again by ourselves, walking on the road without purpose or destination, white banners firmly tied to our skulls. We do not really believe that these pieces of banners we are carrying or wearing will save us if rebels see us! We are wearing tattered clothes covering our bodies emaciated by hunger, fatigue and everyday worries. If rebels see us, they will immediately recognize us as refugees. While walking, we are quietly and unconsciously praying that no military vehicle passes by.

After traveling about fifty meters, just before the intersection of Avenue du Congo and Avenue Libération, we see an old man in the shade of a tree, watching us furtively. He is the sentry of an administrative building located on the right. He seems surprised when he sees us moving toward him. Approaching him, we feel that he will scream alerting neighbors. When we arrive in front of him, my mother greets him and right away asks him if he can hide us. He opens his eyes wide and thinks for several seconds looking at us from hair to toes.

After a few moments of thinking, he agrees out of pity to hide us. He quickly looks at both ends of the road to make sure no one saw us, and then he invites us to follow him behind the building that he watches. He gives us water to drink and use to wash. He also gives us clothes to replace the tattered ones we are wearing. And to complete his charitable work, he gives us rice fried in palm oil. This meal of seasoned rice with oil and salt tastes bitter because it has been several months since we have eaten such food.

It is about one in the afternoon. We just finished eating and we are settled into a safe place. The old man eventually tells us his name is Samuel or Sami and he begins to ask us questions. He speaks good French. We start telling him our story, how we left our home in Kigali, Rwanda, how we separated from the other members of our family and especially how we ended up here before him. After listening to this long story, the old man goes from pity to sadness, then to anger. Whenever we hear the purring engine of a vehicle, we stop talking until the vehicle is gone. Every half hour, Samuel leaves the building and goes outside on the road to see what is going on, and then he comes back to inform us.

Several hours pass. The sun finally disappears concluding a horrible day. It is now about six in the evening. As night comes, Samuel tells us that he must take us to the family of his friend because we cannot stay here at his workplace which is also his home.

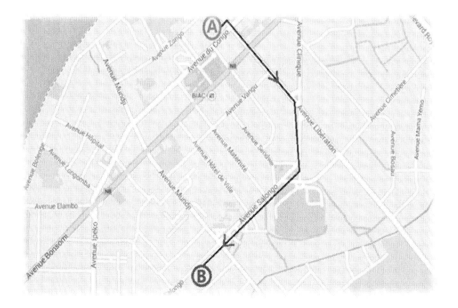

Going to our future home

He takes us with him, and we head north on Avenue du Congo; then we take a right on Avenue Libération. After walking about ten minutes, we are on the long Avenue Salongo.

A dark night without moon and stars covers the entire town. We are moving quickly and quietly, bumping into each other because we can barely see. We do not meet anyone. Whenever we hear a car approaching, we hide behind trees or behind something along the road and wait for the vehicle to pass.

We pass near the Higher Institute of Rural Development (ISDR); we cross the road that extends all the way to Mbandaka. Then we plunge into a dark and narrow street invaded by the bush. A hundred yards away, we leave this road and we head toward a small house almost covered by tall grass.

New residence for the next year and half

A glimmer of an oil lamp hardly dispels the darkness that prevails. The barking of two dogs suddenly pierces the silence of the night. Alerted and worried, the occupants of the house stay on their guard because they know they have visitors. They panic, wondering who would dare to visit them at this hour of the night following a horrible and gruesome day! Apparently our guide Samuel did not notify this family that he was coming. Seeing four silhouettes approaching slowly, the two dogs, Jack and Drompe bark louder until someone calms them down. Samuel mutters something in a language we never heard before. We understand he just presented himself. As soon as we cross the threshold of the house, an old woman turns up the wick of the lamp to see us a little more clearly and to better stare at us. At first a man greets us, then an old woman and finally a young teenager. All three are scrutinizing us from head to toe and lingering on our faces which are darkened by fear. They are staring at us as if we are aliens. Four old stools are brought out, and we are invited to sit down. Samuel, who brought us here, engages in a long speech for about twenty minutes in their dialect. Out of everything he says, we grasp the word *Rwandese* which is repeated and we conclude that he is introducing us or talking about us to these people. As they talk they look at us from time to time. As for us, we are silent. We are reviewing the events of this day which is ending. We are wondering what is going to happen to us. The long speech finally comes to an end. They turn simultaneously toward us. We are brought back from our deep thoughts by Samuel's deep and harsh voice. He is asking us to enter the house. Our guests show us a modestly furnished room. In the dim light of a candle, we see a little bench and three old chairs with torn and ripped cushions. We enter the room and we let ourselves be cradled by these old chairs. Samuel comes into the room and says goodbye to us, shaking our hands. He pulls the door shut behind him. We hear the sound of his footsteps fading as he moves away.

After his departure, silence falls. But we can still hear some confused whisperings through the door. A few minutes later, the door cracks, yawns and the young man appears with two large plates in his hands. He places them before us, disappears and reappears with a basin containing a little water. He wants to wish us a good appetite, but not knowing what language we speak, he gives up and disappears, with a sharp crack of the old wooden door. Some of the food he just brought to us, we have never seen before. On the first plate is a red sauce covering grilled fish. On the second plate there are five large pieces of boiled fruits we have never seen before.

Our first meal: Breadfruit

After hesitating a moment, we decide to eat the fruit because if they brought them for us to eat, that means they are edible. These fruits, tasting like potatoes, are local products called Momboya (breadfruit).

Chapter 22

First miserable weeks in Mbandaka

We spend the first week in this small room that becomes our prison. Each night, they bring us in here. We leave the room only in the evening or at night to take a shower and use the bathroom. If one of us has to go to the toilet during the day, we need to call someone who will first check outside and make sure no one can see us. When visitors come to visit this family, they sit outside, eat, feast, laugh with our hosts and leave without realizing that we are hidden in here, behind the wall, locked in a room where we spend all days and nights sleeping until our ribs start hurting. For us, there is not a difference between day and night. We are told that it is for our good and safety that we must remain hidden for several days or weeks.

Our first weeks with this host family are painful. I become traumatized and almost all my nights are haunted by nightmares. In my nightmares I often see one or more people coming towards me, guns in hands to kill me. I shout, calling for help, until my mother wakes me up holding me in her arms. Our hosts are starting to get tired of these repetitive sessions of my waking up almost every night screaming. They end up bringing an octogenarian traditional healer who heals me. Days later I learn that he is found dead in a cemetery. My little sister is struck by an inexplicable disease that at gnaws her slowly. She loses human appearance. She desperately consumes different kinds of modern drugs that become her daily food. She switches to traditional medicines. Different kinds of wild plants and herbs are brought to her. One day, she falls into a coma and eventually her heart stops beating. We are all alone at home. My mother sends me to tell a Catholic nun who lives in the neighborhood that my little sister just passed away. She was a friend of our host family and she knew about us. When this nun passes the bad news to her other nun sisters, they begin whispering; "Now these neighbors have hidden Rwandese refugees in their home. How will they explain this?" After hearing what they are saying, I go back home to inform my mother. When I arrive, I find my mother in conversation with my sister whose voice barely can he heard. I am seized with fear. The nun eventually comes accompanied by two old women.

A month later, we have begun to get out of the room and stay outside, but out of sight of people passing by. If they see us, they can betray our presence. But we know that one cannot hide a house built on a mountain. We are eventually seen by neighbors and visitors and are later betrayed. To be able to get out of the house and go on the road in front of the house, we had to wait two months.

Gradually, we start learning Lingala which is the local language in order to be able to communicate with the people around us.

As life slowly resumes its course for us, things are changing politically. The country has fallen into the hands of rebels who have changed the flag, the national anthem and the name of the country. The country's new authorities agree with local leaders from several localities to look for hidden Rwandese refugees. We learn that a search for refugees will be organized in several houses in the town of Mbandaka. Refugees who are found will be handed to the High Commissioner for Refugees, who is said to be ready to take them home to Rwanda. Our hosts, already informed, explain the situation to us and make the decision that we must hide in the bush behind the house for the entire day that the search will last. My mother, sister and I spend the whole day sitting there in the bush which is full of mosquitoes, without eating or drinking.

Weeks and months go by and we are used to our neighbors, and we often draw water from their wells. Many people know us. Few are those who like or love us and many hate us without knowing why.

Chapter 23

The first UNHCR agent pays us a surprise visit

While our hosts are gone to work, to the market and/or to school, we have a surprise visit from an officer of the UNHCR (United Nations High Commissioner for Refugees). For us the UNHCR is an enemy. We know that UNHCR in this part of the country is working with Rwanda to send all refugees back to that country. We three are alone at home. I am getting ready to shower when I hear a vehicle pull into the yard.

HCR officer's vehicle

It is a white Land Cruiser, an off-road vehicle with a blue UNHCR sign. I feel my heart beating faster and fear runs through my whole body because I understand what this means. The idea of jumping through the window and running away through the bush comes into my mind, but something holds me back. A dark skinned man, of medium height, wearing blue jeans, gets out of the car. My mother and my little sister, motionless on the porch, feel the earth collapsing under our feet when we see him approaching. He walks slowly, taking his time and looking at the onion and eggplant rows lining the garden on both sides of the driveway. I am doing my best to conceal myself in the small, dark shower room. When he gets near my mother and sister, he greets them in Kinyarwanda, our native language. Stunned, my mother does not say a word. She wonders if he is a friend who wants to surprise her or an enemy who wants to trap her.

Thinking that she did not hear him, the agent repeats his greeting so loud and so clearly that even a deaf person would have heard it. Once again, he grows silent waiting for a reply from my mother. Staring at my mother, with a nervous smile, the officer continues in our native language: «I am greeting you. Why aren't you saying anything? Are you pretending you do not understand what I am saying? I know very well that you are Rwandese refugees; do not tell me otherwise. «Feeling unveiled, disarmed and betrayed, my mother decides to reply to him in our language: "Your guide got the wrong house! We are not Rwandese! We are displaced Congolese from Bukavu." Bukavu is a town in eastern Congo, located on the border of Rwanda. "My father is Congolese from Bukavu and my mother is Rwandese," continues my mother hoping to justify her knowledge of Rwandese language while convincing the agent that she is not Rwandese. In this city of Mbandaka during these first weeks after Rwandese refugee massacres took place here, Rwandese are wanted by the new authorities of this country. They use the UNHCR to find those refugees wherever they are hiding.

The agent does not reply to what my mother just explained. He pretends to believe her but he is not fooled. In every house suspected of hiding refugees, he probably gets the same answer: "We are displaced Congolese from the East!" It is true that eastern Congo has a population that speaks the Rwandese language or a language that is very similar. Therefore, it is not easy to confirm immediately that someone is Rwandese simply because that person speaks Kinyarwanda. So we use this fact to hide ourselves behind a Congolese identity to avoid a forced repatriation or worse. The silence falls and the agent, after scanning the yard, says:

"Where are your hosts?"

"They went out," whispers my mother.

"And your second child, where is he?" (He is talking about me). It is clear that the agent knew about us before coming!

"He is in the shower," replies my mother who starts calling me, inviting me to come and greet someone. From a distance, I tell her that I am coming. I get quietly out of the shower and listen to the whole conversation. As soon as the officer sees me, he quips: «Why didn't you come to greet your uncle?» Without saying anything, I offer him my hand, greet him and go back to hiding in the house.

After a few minutes, he promises my mother to return the next day to meet with our hosts. Through the door of the house, I see him going away, getting in his car and disappearing. Almost terrorized, we believe that he is going to inform soldiers to come pick us up while our hosts are not here. My mother tells me and my sister to hurry up and go hide at our neighbors' because the agent may decide to come right back for us. After he leaves, my mother locks herself in the house. An hour later, one of our hosts returns home and is surprised to find the house quiet. He knocks on the door but no one gives a sign of life. Worried about our absence, he goes to the neighbors' to ask if they saw us and then he sees us. My little sister and I are hiding behind the neighbors' house. We tell him what happened. We return with our host to the house and my mother opens the door after we identify ourselves.

As promised, the UNHCR officer returns the next day and finds one of our hosts in the garden. After seeing his car approaching, my mother, my sister and I rush into the house. We do not come out until a quarter of an hour later, after the departure of the agent.

Our host, having accompanied the officer to his car, returns and explains the situation to us: «He tells me that the UNHCR is sending back to Rwanda all Rwandese refugees hidden in Mbandaka. He advises me to hand you guys to the UNHCR, but I explained to him that you do not want to return to Rwanda. Fortunately, he finally asked me for a bribe in order to conceal you. He will tell his superiors that he has been misinformed, that you are not Rwandese but displaced Congolese.»

Chapter 24

Getting used to life in Mbandaka

Months pass. We have started to freely circulate through the town of Mbandaka. People easily recognize us as Rwandese refugees and some of them laugh at us, humiliate us and sometimes children insult us for no reason. To earn money, I start selling small bags of iced water at the port and in the markets.

Iced water I sold

Every morning I go to our neighbors' house to get the iced water that I had put in small bags in the refrigerator the night before. I put the bags in a big cooler that I carry on my head all the way to the port where I start selling them shouting in Lingala: "Cold water! Cold water! Here is cold water!» When days are sunny and warm, or when commercial boats or ships from Kinshasa and Kisangani arrive at the port, it is my lucky day because I make money by selling hundreds of bags of water.

The sad thing about it is that every evening I have to give three quarters of the money I have earned to our hosts. I use what I have left to buy clothes and shoes for us.

One day my mother meets an old woman from Belgium who has been living in Mbandaka for decades. My mother tells her about our situation and the difficulties we experience every day. The woman decides to hire my mother as a housekeeper at first and then a few weeks later she promotes her to seamstress in her sewing shop.

In October 1998, our host family decides to register me and my little sister in school.. Since we consider ourselves to be displaced Congolese and not Rwandese, we need to register in school with Congolese names. Our host family gives us their family name. This will be a problem later on when we will decide to take back our Rwandese names. All of our birth certificates, identification papers and school papers will have our Congolese names. After my primary education in the elementary school of Mbandaka, I pass the exam to enter high school. The Belgian woman, for whom my mother works, decides to enroll me at the Institut des Frères Iro, one of the best high schools in the town of Mbandaka. It is said that the President Mobutu, recently deposed, may have attended this high school. As for my sister, this woman removes her from the small primary school that she attends and enrolls her at Ecole Belge of Mbandaka, a Belgian school attended by white children and children of rich. This is a great change for us! Finally we are starting to have hope in life. As for our host family and neighbors, hatred and jealousy arise. They ask each other: «How come these refugees that we just saved from the snares of death and from the streets are attending these good schools that even our children have never had the chance to attend?» The young man in our host family, barely a teenager, does not like school. When the host's children see us every morning, my little sister and I going to school and my mother going to work, they become exasperated.

From this moment our host family and neighbors start hating us. This family starts requiring us to do all of the domestic work and especially the hard work in the garden.

Every day, early in the morning before going to school or late in the evening after school, I have to go deep into the bush looking for cooking firewood. The bush is so thick that even people in our host family are afraid to go there alone. I have no choice but to comply. If I refuse, they may evict us from the house and we have nowhere to go. Each morning my sister and I have to get up early and go into the garden to pick leeks whose pungent odor attracts mosquitoes that bite us everywhere. After picking the leeks, I have to sell them at markets that are located two or three kilometers away. Then I come home and start getting ready to go to school. Too bad for me if I get to school late. But I do my best not to be late and to get to school before the gate closes at eight o'clock in the morning.

More than a year passed when one day the UNHCR appears in our lives again. This time, a reward has been promised to those who will finger hidden Rwandese refugees who managed to escape the massacres, the search and repatriation.

Money reward for reveling refugees' hiding place

Authorities of the country and officers of UNHCR know very well that there are still Rwandese refugees in this town of Mbandaka. They are trying to bring them out of their hiding places. This is a strategy put in place by the new regime in Rwanda. They want to bring all refugees back to Rwanda so that they can do to them whatever they want. Many people, including our neighbors, know, think or have heard that we are Rwandese refugees. So we are not surprised one morning when we see another UNHCR vehicle pulling into our backyard. A UNHCR agent gets out of the car followed by two young men.

HCR second officer's vehicle

The agent walks toward the house while the two young people, that we immediately recognize, lean against the car to see what will happen.

«Hello,» the agent says when he gets to the porch where the head of our host family is sitting.

The agent says:

"You are the owner of the house?"

"Yes, of course," says our host.

"I came as part of UNHCR project to visit the Rwandese refugees who are under your roof," continues the agent.

"Under my roof? Here? I think, Mr. Agent, you have been misinformed."

"No, sir, I am pretty sure that you are hosting three Rwandese refugees: a mother and her two children."

"They are not Rwandese sir; one moment," says our host getting up and entering the house. A minute later he returns with a couple of papers in his hands.

"Look! You will see for yourself that they are not Rwandese refugees," says our host, handing the papers to the agent.

"The agent takes a huge pair of glasses from his pocket, puts them on and reads the papers.

"Since when did they arrive?"

"I . . . I think it was late 1996," mumbles our host.

"That should be right," acknowledges the agent after reading everything that is scribbled on the papers "because Rwandese refugees arrived in May 1997. Anyway," he adds, "I apologize for disturbing you; surely these young men were wrong!"

"So those . . . thank you . . . good day! That is alright, it is part of the job I am sure," says our host.

The agent returns to his vehicle and tells the young curious bystanders: «Let's go back; you are mistaken.» They insist but the agent, upset for wasting his precious time, invites them to get in the vehicle. He probably will abandon them somewhere on the street because they are not useful anymore. These young people were right, but they did not have proof! So they just missed whatever reward they expected to receive for our three heads! Our host had done the necessary thing to get us papers certifying that we are displaced Congolese from Bukavu and not Rwandese refugees.

Days, weeks and months pass. We start discovering one by one other Rwandese refugees who, being hidden too long, are starting to come out of their hiding place just like us. The number of Rwandese refugees who come out of hiding in Mbandaka is at first ten, then fifty and later more than a hundred.

Chapter 25

New rebellion in eastern Congo
(Second Congo War)

New rebellion in eastern Congo

We are approaching the end of 1998. While the Congolese population is still getting used to the new regime of Laurent Désiré Kabila, military boots are once again heard in the eastern Congo announcing the beginning of the Second Congo War. Barely a year and a half after the new regime comes to power, a new rebellion begins gnawing the country from the East at an incredible pace. Immediately, Rwandese people are singled out for participating in this new war or for being behind it. It is official that the four-year-old Kigali regime is among many countries who are directly or indirectly involved in this new war which aims to overthrow the new regime of President Laurent Désiré Kabila in the Congo. The situation seems to be reversed for him. The friends who helped him conquer this huge country two years earlier are the ones attacking him.

In Mbandaka authorities want to react to the situation. The governor of the province organizes a meeting, and those who attend it report to us that a hunt for all Rwandese people has been initiated because they are accused of being behind the new war. From that moment this slogan was born: «Tikanyoka, boma Rwandais,» meaning «Leave snake, kill Rwandese.» We later learn that because of these meetings and calls for hunting Rwandese, many Rwandese people, refugees and non-refugees are horribly burned with tires and killed. Many killings happened in the capital Kinshasa.

From the day of this meeting given by the governor of the region of Mbandaka, our host family forbids us to cross the porch of the house. Our school and the work for my mother are impossible since we can no longer leave the house.

A few days after a meeting against Rwandese people, some intellectuals and Rwandese student refugees in Mbandaka reportedly request a meeting with the governor or his representatives. During the meeting, the intellectuals and Rwandese student refugees explain: «The Rwandese people here in Mbandaka are refugees. You probably know under what conditions they arrived and lived here in your town. You know how these Rwandese refugees were prosecuted and killed by the current Rwandese regime that seeks to exterminate them! But how could you be confused about them? How could you put all of them in the same banished boat? Many of them are victims just as Congolese people are now . . . « Those who had received them came to understand, but it was already too late. They could do nothing. They could not reorganize the meeting. But I know that the people of Mbandaka were kind to us refugees because no Rwandese refugee, to my knowledge, was killed in Mbandaka because of that meeting. Maybe they did not want to defile themselves with the blood of poor and miserable people. Soldiers in Mbandaka later sang in a training song: «Batu nani Nzambe Apimela bomengo? Ba Rwandais Nzambe Apimela bomengo!» meaning «What people God has deprived of happiness? Rwandese people God has deprived of happiness!"

The new rebellion continues its conquest of the country. Increasing rumors of insecurity add to the suffering that we are enduring every day in our host family's home. Life becomes more and more difficult for us. Seeing themselves how much they are abusing us, our host family members are starting to think that with the little money that my mother was able to save so far, we will escape. They are certainly right. The host family had started to use us as slaves because they saved and helped us.

Chapter 26

Departure from Mbandaka

For the last few days, we have been preparing to leave this house and this family for good. One afternoon, while all of the host family members are gone, we pick up all our belongings and leave. We first go to stay for a couple of days with two Rwandese sisters in town that we met a few weeks earlier. They are renting a small house in the suburbs. The host family that we escaped soon learns where we are staying after asking around. When they ask us to come back, we nicely thank them for all the good they have done for us and tell them that we have decided to live by ourselves.

As the new rebellion approaches our town, we are afraid that this time the rebels will not leave us alive. This rebellion is partially composed of the same people who were in the previous rebellion that chased us and tried to kill us a year and a half earlier. This situation causes my mother, my sister and me to make the decision to leave Mbandaka as soon as possible just like other Rwandese refugees are doing. About two weeks before our departure, UNHCR officials who are not our enemies anymore, inform us that they have located and even met my twin sister from whom we were separated long ago and far away. They tell us that they found her on an island which requires two days of sailing to reach. They could not bring her before talking to her hosts who were then absent. They assure us that we will be able to see her in a few days.

Today is our scheduled departure day. My twin sister is still not here. We have been waiting for her for a week and half! We waited for the UNHCR staff members to return from looking for her so that we can leave town together, but they keep repeating to us the same thing: «We do not have enough fuel for the boats and we do not yet have an agent available to go look for her.» We do know that the island is far away (a two-day trip by boat), but we do not think that they are doing their best. And besides we are not even sure it is her. Yet rumors are spreading that rebels might attack Mdandaka at any moment. We are afraid and running out of patience. We have to make a choice now: either stay and wait for my supposed sister or leave today. My mother tells us that if we stay here waiting for her, we could all die, and the UNHCR staff members could be lying to us in order to divert us from our intention of leaving the town. (They already know about it.) With sorrow, we decide to leave without her, commending her to God's care.

It is in the evening of Tuesday December 21, 1998. After a year and a half, we leave this town of Mbandaka. Around five-thirty in the evening, while the enormous sun disappears at the horizon, we board a large boat going to Congo Brazzaville, the neighboring country.

Crammed in a boat

Throughout the night, the boat in which we are crammed with merchants and their goods navigates down the Congo River until morning. The three of us: my mother, my sister and I are the only Rwandese people on board this boat. But we are not afraid because this time we paid our boat fare just like everybody else and we are not so badly dressed as to attract attention. For curious people who ask us, we tell them that we are going to join our families in the Congo.

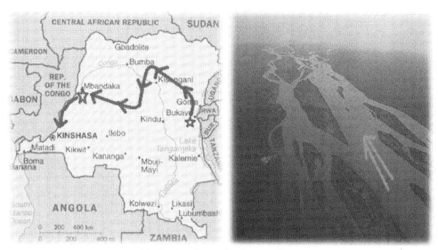

Navigating down the Congo River

We spend the following day navigating the Congo River. In the evening, we do not stop until we reach a small market center where fishermen and locals come to sell fish and exchange goods.

The next morning, we switch boats and board one going to the border of the Congo where we should arrive by the evening. Throughout the day, we continue heading south navigating through the waters of the great Congo River, gazing at the small and often uninhabited islands that seem to be moving on our left and right. It is amazing to see all this great area of the country where there is only water. No roads, no vehicles.

Still in water

Roads are replaced by the rivers while vehicles are replaced by boats. In order to buy something at the market or to visit family or friends, people take boats! Children spend their days playing in the water with tiny boats. People eat fish day after day, month after month. Even a three-year-old child already knows how to catch a fish.

Chapter 27

Abandoned on a small island

In the evening, we eventually reach the coast of the Republic of Congo. We are preparing to get off the boat and set our feet on the Congolese soil when Congolese authorities in the coastal town of Ndjondu refuse us entry to the country after learning that we are Rwandese refugees. In this locality, there is already a camp of Rwandese refugees, but we do not understand yet why we have been refused entry. Some of those who have seen us being refused entry to the territory try to negotiate with the authorities so that they will grant us entry. We are still waiting in the boat. As night approaches, the boatmen who brought us want to depart but they do not know where to leave us. They do not have time to wait for our situation to be determined by the authorities. Out of patience for the seemingly endless negotiations, the boatmen turn the boat around to go back to the Democratic Republic of Congo that we just left. There are five people in the boat: my mother, my sister, the two boatmen and I. We ask them where they are taking us, but we do not get an answer. We are starting to panic. When we arrive at something that looks like an island in the middle of nowhere, the boatmen stop and ask us to get off their boat. When we ask them why they want to leave us in this place, they angrily respond that they are in a hurry and that we just have to get off the boat before they use force.

Lonely Island

We finally decide to get off the boat. The mist preceding the night is already covering the big river before enveloping this little island where we just got abandoned. Hearing the sound of the old YAMAHA engine of the boat that left us behind, about seven people, probably the inhabitants of this island, come in our direction and gather around us. Among them is a mature man in his forties, a woman traditionally dressed, a teenager girl and children. The head of the family, who immediately recognizes us as Rwandese refugees, greets us in French and asks us what we are doing here. We explain to him what just happened. He immediately confesses to us that he does not like Rwandese people. After humbly asking him why, he starts telling us a story: «When I was traveling more than a year ago, I met with a young Rwandese refugee man fleeing war going to Congo, just like you guys. He pleased me and I felt pity for him. He did not know where he was going and he did not have any family member left with him. I was very moved when he told me his story from the time he was in his family of twelve people till that day when I meet him alone. I then decided to hide him with me and offer him the warmth of a family. He became like my son and I was going with him in my field and fishing. I even had promised him the hand of my eldest daughter that you see here! When peace came, for reasons that I still do not understand, he decided to leave without even saying goodbye.» We understand the decision of the young man he told us about because we just spent over a year in a similar situation. But we admit to him that the young man was definitely disrespectful toward him! Many Rwandese children, women and men are still in the most remote areas of the Congo, serving their rescuers who might have "bewitched" them after they told them they wanted to go home and join their countrymen or their families. This is why, unfortunately, many refugees preferred not to inform their host families of their intentions to leave. They fear being prevented from leaving.

We try to make this man forget about this story so that we can find favor in his eyes because our life on «his» island currently depends on his and his family's goodwill. A few minutes later, the man shows us a place under trees which will shelter us for the night. He warns us that there are a lot of mosquitoes on this island.

Annoyed by mosquitoes that are already beginning to bite us everywhere, we are preparing to squeeze ourselves inside a tiny mosquito screen protector that we just set up when the man's wife appears with a basket in her hands. In the basket are some freshly caught fish, still faintly breathing and struggling. They caught these fish for us after noticing that we were going to sleep without eating. The fish soon land in the pot and into our bellies some thirty minutes later. After the tasty fish meal, we fall into deep slumber.

Every morning that we spend on this lonely island, our host and his daughter come to ask us if we spent a good night. «Very good,» we always respond despite the cold and mosquitoes that devour us every night. Every day, the family brings us fresh fish for our daily food. Without this good family, I do not know how we would have survived on this island because apparently fish is the only food here and we do not know how to fish and even if we did, we have no fishing tools. A true friendship starts forming between us and this solitary, nice and friendly family. We realize that maybe humans often live happier when they are alone in nature, far from their peers who are often the source of problems and conflicts.

Rwandese refugees that I mentioned at the beginning of this chapter, who were negotiating on our behalf in order for us to be granted entry into the Congo, are probably and hopefully still negotiating with authorities because we really do not see a future for us on this island.

Chapter 28

Departure to the Republic of the Congo

A long week just ended and we are still here on the island. We are slowly getting used to the life here. This morning we are sitting on the edge of the river contemplating that forbidden Congolese territory on the other side of the river. We are admiring the beautiful rising sun that gives the impression of rising from water on the horizon. We are listening to the soft trickling of water in the river and the beautiful melodies of birds which are swimming and singing at the beginning of another beautiful day. From a distance, we see at the horizon, on the large expanse of river water, a small point that is growing.

Looking at the forbidden territory

Minutes later, the point has grown into a large boat floating on the water and two men are inside. The two strong paddlers advance towards us, rowing as if they are following a rhythm of an inaudible anthem. We run toward them as if we know they are bringing us good news.

These two men are Rwandese refugees who, after lengthy greetings, tell us that they came to take us. Without wasting time, we immediately pack our bags. Our host family on the island has gathered around us to say goodbye. With tears in our eyes, we deeply thank them for their warm welcome and the unforgettable hospitality in their little world. A few minutes later, we are navigating away from the island which is becoming smaller behind us.

After an agitated crossing caused by the wind blowing over the big river, we finally set foot on the territory of the Republic of Congo. We are warmly welcomed by our countrymen waiting for us on the shore. Here, there is a large Rwandese refugee camp. My mother meets old friends that she knew back in our country. Despite the modestly and poorly constructed tents, people seem to live peacefully and harmoniously with the local population.

Ndjondo refugee camp

A few hours after our arrival, we learn that other Rwandese refugees are in areas to the north. Since this camp is very close to the Congo Kinshasa that we just left behind, we will not feel safe here. We want to go as far as possible from this Congo Kinshasa in which we have suffered for the past four years of our lives.

The same day we meet new Rwandese refugees who tell us their stories which are as interesting as ours. But we are particularly interested in a Rwandese refugee who came from Enyellé, one of those remote villages in the north of the country, housing few tens of Rwandese refugees. This gentleman had come south looking for his wife and two children. He was told that they were seen in one of the Rwandese refugees' camps located in the southeast of this country. Unfortunately, he found no one and he is on his way back. After we ask several questions about the village in which he lives and the life there, we decide to embark with him the next morning so that he can guide us to that village of Enyellé.

Chapter 29

Almost two weeks spent in water, on a ship

The next day early in the morning, we are awakened by the foghorn of a cargo ship that must stop here for a few hours before continuing to sail north.

First day on the ship

In the afternoon the ship sails and we are on board. We are near the end of December, in the region's dry season. The water is so low that most large ships have suspended their traffic in these waters, as is customary at this time of year. This cargo ship constantly gets stuck in the sand or hits rocks on the bottom of the river. The rocks are only a couple of meters below the surface of the water. This ship is supposed to carry only oil and gasoline, but it is often used to transport goods and passengers. We are forbidden from making a cooking fire on top of some containers, rail cars or barges that contain flammable liquids.

Still in water

The ship full of people and goods starts sailing north, along the banks of the Congo River which becomes Oubangui River when continuing toward north.

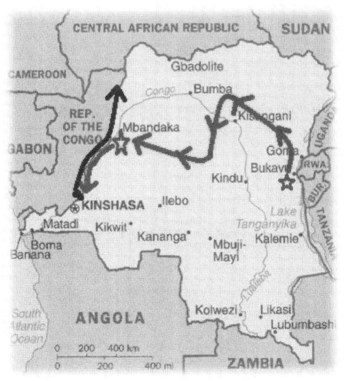

Navigating toward north

We have been on the ship for two days, and it is barely moving because it is navigating against the current. The ship also zigzags to avoid under water rocks and shallow places. Every time the ship hits a rock and gets stuck in the sand, we have to stop for hours. The ship is also stopping several times at different coastal commercial centers dropping off and/or picking up passengers, merchants and goods.

On the fifth day, an unusual sun heats the region we are navigating. The boat has only one small roof for shelter against the sun, the captain's cabin. I am reminded that this boat is normally not intended to carry passengers but flammable liquids. This means that there is no place for passengers and their goods to take shelter against the sun, wind or rain. The iron barges or containers of oil and gasoline are heated, and liquids inside begin to evaporate to the point that we believe that the ship will catch fire.

Very hot day on the ship

Worse yet we cannot even walk or sit on those hot iron containers. We have no choice other than sitting on our bags and covering ourselves with clothes until the evening when the sun sets.

Three days later, on our eighth day on the ship, suddenly the sky is covered with heavy and dark clouds behind which the sun flees. A storm followed by a torrential rain befalls us. Many of our bags on the containers are swept into the water by the wind.

Caught in a storm on the ship

The ship, despite its size and weight, swings under the power of the wind to the point that we are afraid it will overturn. To hide from this furious storm and heavy rain, we are all invited to go down and squeeze ourselves inside the empty oil or gasoline containers. In here, it is dark and hard to breathe because there are so many of us and there is only one small opening for air and light. While it is raining outside, we are hot inside the containers! We stay confined here for a long hour until the storm calms down. The next day, we continue traveling on the Oubangui River, passing by the town of Impfondo.

The first day of 1999 finds us in this ship where we spent almost two weeks before being left on shore at a deserted village. The ship continues its ascent of the river toward Bangui.

Chapter 30

Toward the locality of Enyellé

The boat leaves us near a trail along the river. The trail extends a distance of about ten kilometers. Without wasting time, we travel the ten kilometers on foot before reaching the village called Boyélé, along the Oubangi River, several hours later. We are still with our guide who informs us that since today is the market day, we have a chance of reaching the village of Enyellé by the evening.

On certain days of the week, this locality of Boyélé is a small village and some other days it becomes a big market where there is a gathering of sellers, buyers, thieves and beggars, some of whom come from distant regions.

Village of Boyelé

About three in the afternoon, sellers and buyers begin returning home to wait for the next market day. A truck that brought merchants from Enyellé is getting ready to return. After paying our fares to the driver, we climb in the back of the truck with our bags. Most of the passengers are women who came to the market. The old truck barely starts, but it proceeds along a narrow, dusty and bumpy road. We learn that our destination is about fifty kilometers away. The trip will take us a little over an hour.

In the truck heading to Enyellé

An hour and thirty minutes later, we reach Enyellé covered with dust. Since we are not used to this kind of trip, we are hurting everywhere because of the bumpy road.

New destination

   We are welcomed by a few Rwandese refugees who have lived here for some time. The first thing we learn is that life is hard in this big village. We soon start experiencing it. In the first weeks, my mother, sister and I are hosted by a Christian family. We learn that to earn money, most refugees draw water for the local population who pay them. That is what waited for me. I soon start looking for families to work for by providing them with water for a small sum of money. Three days after our arrival, I have already started making money. Every morning, I go in different families asking them if they need someone to fetch water. They give me a big, empty, twenty-five liter container that I have to bring back full of water for a pay of 100 CFA francs, local currency (about € 0.10 or $ 0.15 in those days).

25-liter containers used to make money

The water source is located approximately two kilometers in the bottom of the valley, in the middle of the bush. I have to descend the steep slopes in order to get to the water source and come back up the hill with the container full of water on my head.

The source of water

To earn more money I have to make several rounds per day, providing water to different families. Many other poor people in this village do the same work in order to earn money and support their families.

Poor women doing the same job as mine

I manage to save a bit of money. A month later my mother adds my money to what she has and rents a small shop where we will live and start selling small things such as candies, chewing gum and cigarettes. The only economic activity in this village is a wood processing plant located a few kilometers from the village. I start going there from time to time trying to get temporary work such as collecting and transporting pieces of wood, waste etc. For a few hundred CFA francs a day - CFA is local currency. I also give a hand to those who make charcoal. Two months later, when life starts smiling on us again, my mother decides that my sister and I should enroll in school.

It has been three months since we arrived here in Enyellé, north of the Republic of Congo, in January 1999. The southern part of the country, near the capital Brazzaville, is ruled by organized guerilla forces that remain loyal to Lissouba, former President of the Congo overthrown by Sassou Nguesso's coup in 1997, two years earlier. Once again Rwandese people or refugees are involved in this war ravaging this other Congo. Rumors say that young Rwandese living here in this village of Enyellé are going to be forcibly recruited by the rebel movement or the government to fight while other rumors say that Rwandese young people will be killed by the rebels or the government because they are accused of helping the enemy. In all this frightening and confusing political instability, we do not feel safe once again. Whatever will come out of this situation will not be good for me, my mother and sister. We have to get out of here and go somewhere else. My mother explains our situation and concern to a neighbor Congolese woman who informs us that she travels almost every weekend to Bangui, the capital of the neighboring country called Central African Republic. She has family there. My mother already sees it as an opportunity! The woman promises to help us whenever we decide that we want to get out of here. We will not wait months to jump on this opportunity. In only one week, we are prepared to leave!

Chapter 31

Departure to Bangui, Central African Republic

One evening in April 1999, around five o'clock, we climb into the back of a commercial truck full of people going to Bangui to buy or sell goods. We are with the neighbor woman who will guide us all the way to her family in Bangui.

On road for Bangui

About four hundred and fifty kilometers separate us from Bangui. The day is already declining when the heavy vehicle starts traveling the first kilometers of this long trip. This remote region of the country has few inhabitants and few roads. There is only one narrow, long, dusty main road through this vast forest area. The passage of the truck with the deafening noise of the old engine attracts many Pygmy families and their children. They leave their huts and stand on the edge of the road to greet us and watch us cross their little world.

Pygmy's population on roadside

These Pygmies who are almost the only people living in this green region of the country are starting to feel threatened by the progressive deforestation. The long road which we are traveling traverses a vast forest that covers the northern part of the Congo; the road crosses the border and extends over tens of kilometers into Central African territory.

New destination

The vehicle's strong lights pierce the darkness formed by the branches of the giant trees that almost cover the road. Strong gusts of cold wind freeze the blood in our veins. The driver of the truck traveling at about ninety kilometers per hour has forgotten that we are not sitting on chairs but on wood. He does not slow down to reduce the violent jolts caused by the bumpy road.

About ten at night, the vehicle slows down and stops at a gate. We are told that we are on the border between two countries. The border patrol asks us to show our identification papers. Half an hour later, we hit the road again for a little while. After traveling a few kilometers, the truck breaks down and the driver decides to pull to the side of the road here in the middle of the night and in the middle of the forest. Taking advantage of this little break, we fall asleep. It is totally silent except for the sounds of nocturnal birds and animals.

Two hours later we are awakened by the sudden start of the truck. We are back on the road and we are almost flying. We soon reach a paved road, wide and deserted. The driver burns up the road causing the speedometer needle to reach a hundred and twenty kilometers an hour. At three in the morning, we are at the entrance of the capital city of Bangui where we decide to stop and spend the rest of the long night.

The date is April 25, 1999. We are awakened from our short sleep around six in the morning by a crowd of people going to or coming from the city of Bangui. We can already smell the polluted air of the city. When we get on the road again, entering the suburbs of Bangui, we think we are entering another world because this is the first time we have entered a capital since we left Kigali, the capital of our country Rwanda, exactly five years ago.

Arriving in Bangui

The truck driver drops us off at Kilomètre Cinq, the largest shopping center in the city. From there, we take the yellow taxi with our guide and the head to her family to the Castor neighborhood. The host family, despite its many problems, manages to spare us a little space to sleep in the living room of their house. And they give us food. In the following days, this host family helps us to find other Rwandese refugees in Bangui. We eventually learn that there is a small temporary camp for refugees in the center of the city, a few kilometers from where we are staying.

Chapter 32

Beginning of a new life in Bangui

After spending a week with this generous family, we decide to join other refugees in the temporary refugee camp at Port Amont, in the downtown area. The camp consists of a hangar in an old, abandoned port for ships at the edge of the Oubangui River. More than a hundred refugees, mostly Rwandese and Congolese, live there. We are allocated a small area on the terrace of a large ,empty warehouse. We are also given some pots, blankets and food. At least the living conditions are better than the jungle. Here we even have Mass every Sunday for those who still believe. A European Catholic priest who was able to learn our language Kinyarwanda comes every Sunday to try to bring hope into our lives again.

Bangui, capital of Central African Republic

A new life is starting for us. I enroll in high school and my little sister enrolls in a primary school. While French is the official language in this country, most of the population speaks Sango, the local language that we must learn to be able to integrate into this new society and culture. Even though we are able to eat, sleep and go to school in peace, the health conditions are bad in this temporary refugee camp. One day a wall collapsed and killed some of the refugee families who thought they had found shelter. This was one of the reasons that led to the facility's closure a few weeks later.

When the UNHCR and/or the authorities decide to close the temporary camp, refugees are invited to join other refugees in a refugee camp located in a remote province of the country. The camp is about tens or even hundreds of kilometers from the city of Bangui. The few days we have to pack our bags allow us to think of what we will do once we arrive in this camp. What is certain is that if we go to this camp, it may be the end of our school attendance. My sister and I rely on getting an education. It is necessary for our future. And if we stay here in the city of Bangui, UNHCR is not going to take care of us anymore because we will be considered local residents and not refugees. It is up to us to weigh the benefits and consequences of staying here in town or going to live in the refugee camp in the province. My mother, my sister and I, together with other refugees decide to stay in the city regardless of the consequences. We have lived in country areas long enough.

A couple of months after our decision to stay in the town of Bangui on our own, my mother gets a job in a local French medical facility. This allows us to rent a small studio in the suburbs of Bangui. My little sister and I get to continue our education. I am fortunate to receive a UNHCR scholarship that is granted to high school and university refugee students so they can continue their education.

I finally enroll in private high school called Lycée Centre Protestant pour la Jeunesse where I spend about six years. For about three years, I walk every morning about six kilometers going to this school and walk another six kilometers in evening returning back home. I am relieved from these long daily walking when I receive a bike donation from Tonino Falaguasta, a Catholic Italian missionary. In 2005, I successfully earn a high school diploma from that school with an emphasis in mathematics and physics.

To earn some money, after receiving my high school diploma, I began to tutor in Mathematics, French, history, geography and science to few Rwandese refugee students into their homes at night or evening after school. Most of these children have difficulty in school and / or parents who are traders or workers who do not have enough time to help them. So every night I go to their homes to help them and they pay me every month.

Centre Protestant pour la Jeunesse (CPJ) High School

Chapter 33

Failed military coup of May 28, 2001 in Bangui

Between 1993 and 2013, the country of Central African Republic is the theater of insecurity and repeated political instabilities. Demonstrations, protestations and strikes of all kinds are part of everyday life for the country's population. Since Rwandese refugees are now part of this population, we must share their daily misery which includes hunger, drought, inflation, the impact of wage arrears, disrupted education and corruption and the list goes on.

In the evening of May 28, 2001, during a Mother's Day celebration, one of the biggest festivals in the country, President Ange Félix Patassé survives a military coup led against him by André Kolingba, former president of the country between 1981 and 1993. He might also have been responsible for the protestations and strikes that the country experienced in the decade after his failure in the presidential election of 1993 which was won by President Patassé.

The coup is particularly devastating for the Rwandese refugees' community living in Bangui because it leaves us in mourning. The day after the coup, information spreads in town and among the population saying that Kolingba, the author of the failed coup, has Rwandese mercenaries among his soldiers. This is frightening news for the low class populations who are not even sure whether it is true; the news is not well received by the local population who start showing hostility towards us, Rwandans. Some shops belonging to Rwandese refugees are already being looted while some of their owners are beaten. Some unconfirmed news is saying that some angry local residents are threatening to attack and kill Rwandese people. Fearful of being killed by our neighbors or other angry people, my mother, my sister and I decide to take refuge in the French Institut Pasteur de Bangui facility with a French family my mother works for.

French Institut Pasteur de Bangui facility

We stay there for about a week until we are sure everything has calmed down. Later, we learn that at least three Rwandese people were killed during these events. Life resumes its course with its joys and daily misfortunes.

About two years later, in 2003, the country experiences another military coup led by General François Bozizé against President Ange Félix Patassé. This time, the blow is fatal to the regime of President Patassé who flees the country and goes into exile in Togo. All these insecurities faced by the country worry us more and more. We Rwandese refugees are not alone because this country hosts several thousand refugees from more than ten African countries. The High Commissioner for Refugees (UNHCR), in its attempt to solve refugees' problems in this politically and economically unstable central African country, has programs that assist refugees who want to return to their countries of origin. For refugees who cannot or do not want to return to their countries of origin, the UNHCR assists them with resettlement in other countries. It is in this context that my mother starts the application process for resettlement in another country. This long process will extend over several years during which UNHCR will make inquiries or do investigations into the candidate's country of origin. During this period, the UNHCR will also seek a host country somewhere in the world among countries that are accepting legal, political or war immigrants. The United States is among the countries along with Canada, Australia, Norway, Denmark, New Zealand and the list continues.

Chapter 34

End of the Tunnel

Finally out!

Toward the end of 2006, after seven years of living in Bangui, good news reaches us. The UNHCR informs us that our application for resettlement in another country has led to a good result. We are among refugees selected for political exile in the United States of America, and the beginning of that exile will take place in 2007, the following year. We do not believe it at first! We have had enough surprises, but this is of another kind! It is reality. We are hoping that light will shine in our lives! We do know well that we are not going to heaven, but at least we know that we are going to a place where life is better than the life we have lived since leaving our country in 1994.

Just a few days before our departure, we are informed of which state in America has been chosen for us. Every day that God gives us we have joy about finally leaving, but we also fear another political crisis could ruin everything before we leave. Immense joy overwhelms us. In a way we are sad to leave this country because we lived here for seven long years, but we are also happy to leave it. We made many friends and we have embraced the language and the Central African Republic's culture. Despite all these positive things, something urges us to leave and go far away. We do not feel at home and we do not feel safe. As long as we are here, any disruption in security results in a Rwandese refugee being threatened, beaten, killed or having his shop looted. The military coups, rebellions, insurrections, protestations and strikes experienced by the country between 1994 and 2014 show how this country, the Beautiful Centrafrique is unfortunately one of the most unstable countries in Africa. We have endured enough suffering because of wars.

Chapter 35

Departure to the United States

Our wait finally comes to an end! The date is Wednesday of January 2007 in the morning. We spend about an hour exchanging many goodbyes with long-time neighbors and friends who come to say good-by and wish us the best for our long trip into the future. With our suitcases, we jump in the little yellow taxi that brings us downtown, behind the Port Amont where the UNHCR office is located. More than fifteen other refugees have already arrived. All together more than twenty refugees from different nationalities are scheduled to leave Bangui that day for various destinations in the world. On every face you can see great joy stained with a little anxiety caused by fear of the uncertain future.

During the few minutes we have left before taking the road to the airport, we review the seven years that we spent in this country. We are taking inventory of our past lives and dreaming about our future!

In HCR vehicle to airport

Then, we all are invited to get into these UNHCR vehicles of which we have so many different memories. We immediately start down the road heading to Bangui M'Poko International Airport.

Bangui International Airport

For most of us refugees travelling today, this will be our first time to get on an airplane. We are overwhelmed with joy. Things are going fast. We follow the UNHCR staff members who are doing almost everything for us. After arriving at the airport, we go through security screening, and soon we are invited to board the plane. Our dreams and thoughts prevent us from noticing how late the departure is. Finally, we take off and fly away. Through the small aircraft windows, we can see our past falling behind. The airplane rising into the skies makes us feel light as if the heavy weight of our suffering is falling off. We feel like birds finally escaping from a trap.

The airplane makes a stop about half an hour away in Douala, Cameroon and takes off again heading to Cotonou, the capital of Benin. We reach that destination about two hours after our departure from Bangui. We spend the night in a small hotel in Cotonou. The next morning, we are taken back to the airport to continue our journey.

From Cotonou, we board a large aircraft of the AIRFRANCE Company which will take us to Paris, the capital of France.

Cotonou, Benin to Paris in France

We arrive in Paris the next morning after eight long hours of flying. It is very cold here! In Paris, our group of refugees is divided into small groups according to their destination. My mother, my sister and I stay with a group of refugees flying to the United States. Soon we are again divided into smaller groups according to our various destinations inside the United States. Two hours after our arrival in Paris, our small group is led by an IOM (International Organization for Migration) officer at the departure gate. We board a large transcontinental aircraft belonging to Continental Airlines. This one takes off for Newark Airport, in the State of New Jersey.

Paris to New Jersey

After another eight-hour flight, we land at Newark, in the United States, and this time it is not only cold, but it is snowing! This is our first time to experience snow. We only know of it from books or television. For someone who has never experienced the winter, it is not easy to leave an equatorial climate yesterday and land today in the winter season!

Chapter 36

Final Destination

At Newark, New Jersey, we are welcomed by the immigration office who checks all our immigration and health papers before providing us with documents certifying our refugee status in the US. Our small group is finally dispersed. Now, we are only individual families. We say good-bye to each other while each family is led, still by an IOM officer, to the gate for boarding the airplane to our final destinations in different states. While some families get on planes going to the northern states, others head south and we go westward. Without wasting time, my mother, my sister and I board another Continental airplane that will deliver us, three hours later, at our final destination in Colorado.

New Jersey to Colorado

We arrive at Denver, our final destination at night. It is snowing here too. The trip has taken a total of two days of travel and about twenty-two hours of flight.

We arrive at night. It is snowing here. We are told that we just missed a snow storm a couple of days ago. This explains this bitterness of the cold in which we start our new life in the United States.

Like any beginning, it is difficult for us to adjust to the new culture and American life. We have to learn almost everything all over again starting with the language. We have to start getting used to the local life starting with the harshness of the winter. This new life of ours begins in January 2007. I start by learning English in a local school. Two months later, I get a job in a metallurgical factory where most of my co-workers are Russian. This is my first job in the United States that the refugee settlement agency helps me to obtain. This work consisting of the transforming boiled metals at a very high temperature into other metal shapes is not easy at all. I often go back home with at least one burning somewhere in my hair or on the body. When I get off this hard work in afternoon, I have to take two buses and go to school where I learn English and prepare to retake the high school diploma because the one I received back in Africa in 2005 is in French and it was going to be difficult for me to use it anywhere in US and I did not want to go through the hassle of having it translated every time I will want to use it. I finally obtain the GED three months later, five months after my arrival.

I am particularly grateful to Emily H. and Dave C. who sacrificed their valuable time to help me several times. A year later, I quit my first factory job in order to enroll at a local college and a university where I will start courses in chemistry, mathematics and computer science. I find another job in a hotel where I started as a room cleaner and where I finished five years later as a receptionist after working as a night launderer in the same hotel. Work is not easy for new refugees like me who do not speak English well. But it allows me to discover that sometimes in life you have to start at the bottom level. Then you can better rise without fear of falling back.

A year later, I quit my first factory job in order to enroll at a local college and a university where I will start courses in chemistry, mathematics and computer science. I find another job in a hotel where I started as a room cleaner and where I finished five years later as a receptionist after working as a night launderer in the same hotel. Work is not easy for new refugees like me who do not speak English well. But it allows me to discover that sometimes in life you have to start at the bottom level. Then you can better rise without fear of falling back.

While improving my English skills, I start interpreting for new refugees who speak French, Kinyarwanda, Kirundi, Sango and Lingala. I have been doing that since that day.

In the years that followed, I engage in several different kinds of work and activities such as shopping carts pusher, cashier, math tutor, security guard etc. I get a chance to travel in more than twenty states and Canada discovering the rich variety of American society, climate, population, culture and landscapes.

After five years in the United States, I begin to prepare and study for the test as part of the application in getting American citizenship that allows me to get a job where I start working for the US Federal government.

The long journey

Closing word

This is the end of the major events of this drama that I lived with my family. Many of my Rwandese brothers and sisters lived through similar experiences. Some lived through worse experiences, and of course many died.. I started writing in 2004, ten years after the beginning of the war, in order to share the story with those who want more information about this humanitarian tragedy that struck the Rwandese people. I don't want this story to be used as judgment, condemnation or guilt for anyone or any political or ethnic group. This story serves as a memory for us, and I hope it provides insight for our future generation as we try to avoid another drama of this kind. Let this story bring unity rather than division. Let this story remind us of where we came from and how we got where we are so that we know where we want to go and how to get there.

I got married in 2014 to a former Rwandan refugee who has lived an almost extraordinarily similar experience to mine!

I still live in the same city with my mother and my little sister who live a normal and happier life.

My little sister got married and is now the mother of two beautiful children.

We still do not have news of my twin sister, seventeen years after our separation.

Few years after our separation, we learned that my father and brother were captured by rebels were repatriated back in Rwanda. We are not together, but they are fine where they are.

I thank the

Almighty God

Who preserved us

throughout this hard life experience

and who

still continues to keep his powerful hand on us.

To Him alone be the glory and honor!

Made in the USA
Lexington, KY
30 March 2018